I will not leave you orphans; I will come to you.

—John 14:18

Contents

Foreword

My father was adopted. To say I am grateful for adoption would be an understatement. It was 1936, dad's mother was young, and the pregnancy was not expected. The world was different then. Had it been today, it is likely that my father never would have been born. His mother kept him for several months, but after some time it became clear to her that she was not able to provide my dad the care and type of life that would be best for him. She took him to a group of Catholic nuns who ran an orphanage. Dad was adopted a few months later, an answered prayer to a young couple not able to have children.

My dad was chosen—this is one of the aspects of adoption that moves me most profoundly. In Romans, St. Paul reminds us that we are adopted sons and daughters of God. This raises an interesting question: why did Paul speak of us as being "adopted"? Why not just sons and daughters? Well, in Roman law, you could never abandon a child that you adopted. The thought was that you knew what you were getting, and you could never turn away from your child. You've chosen that child; what a beautiful image of the love between a mother, father, and child.

This is true for modern adoptive parents as well. My grandparents wanted a child but were not able to conceive. They had the tremendous grace of choosing my father, and he was the answer to one of their deepest longings: to have a child they could love, raise, and call their son. I will forever be grateful for their openness to life and for adopting my father.

My dad and I talked quite a bit about his adoption. He always was grateful for his adoptive parents but did wonder about his biological parents. He knew the name of his biological mother and would find out his father's name a few months before he died, but his desire to know was more of a curiosity than a drive to find them. I know that there are some adoptive children who really struggle with this. They may wonder, "Why did my mom give me up for adoption? Why didn't she want me?" I'm sure every situation is different, and there is no easy answer for this, but I was once touched by a conversation I had with an adoptive father. He was able to meet the biological mother of the boy he would adopt. She said to him with tears in her eyes, "The only thing I ask is that you will always let my baby know that I loved him. That's why I am placing him up for adoption. I love him and want him to have a life that I won't be able to give him."

I was so touched by this story. There is something innate about the love of a mother, and, while we won't always know why a mother chooses to make this decision, we do celebrate and thank God that the woman chose life and that a family who longs for a child will have their prayers heard.

Jamie McAleer prayed such a prayer.

I remember the first time Jamie and Jack shared their story of adopting Alexander. It was so beautiful but also something more: it was pure. As they shared their story of how they not only wanted but felt called to adopt a child, I sensed such a goodness about their story. Their intentions were so good, and I was inspired by the passion and drive that had motivated them. Having heard their story many times and having read *I Will Come to You*, I am sure that the reader will also be moved. It is a story of perseverance, trust, a bit of ingenuity, and a whole lot of faith. In the end, *I Will Come to You* is a story of love and faith. It is the story of the love of a husband and wife for God, for each other, for their daughters, and for their son they fought to bring home. In the end, Jamie's story is a testimony to the faithfulness and love of God: He who calls each of us His adopted sons and daughters.

—Fr. Dave Pivonka, T.O.R.

Acknowledgments

The dream of this book has been so long in the making that there is not enough room on this page to thank all the folks who have helped me with their wisdom, insight, and encouragement.

That being said, I must first, with deep gratitude, thank my son-in-law, Philip Martin, a talented writer, gifted teacher, and husband to my daughter Jennifer. Philip sat with me for many hours asking questions and offering suggestions as we pieced together this story of adoption. I wish to thank Dan Johnson, my other son-in-law, a talented director, gifted videographer, and husband to my daughter Lauren, for his creative talent and imagination as well as his encouragement as I struggled to "get this done." Both of these men are gifted storytellers in their prospective mediums who love to touch hearts and turn them toward God.

Much is owed to my friend Fr. Dave Pivonka, who has been such a role model and spiritual guide during my adult life. Thank you for sharing your beautiful words about adoption at the beginning of this book. Most of all, thank you for your friendship.

Thank you, Mary Carey and Michelle Benzinger, for your support and kind words, and Libba Tillman, my sister-in-law, who read this story and gave me her blessing. I also wish to thank

Mike Fontecchio, with Faith and Family Publications, as well as Mike Flickinger and Claire Dwyer for encouraging me and for helping me shape this story into a beautiful book others may read. Thank you, Jacob Smeraglia, for your talent in creating such a beautiful cover.

Once again I thank my daughters, Lauren and Jennifer, as well as my wonderful husband, Jack, for their love and support in achieving my dream of another child, and our son, Alex, for being that dream. Thank you, Laura, for loving and marrying Alex.

Last, but not least, I wish to thank Our Blessed Mother for her support and her maternal love. My continual prayer and desire is that one day I'll be with you and your Son forever.

Introduction

Several years ago, my mother was diagnosed with stage four cancer of unknown primary origin. She really didn't want to fight it or even talk about it. She just wanted to continue living her life as best and happily as she could. At the time, she was in her early eighties, though she didn't look or even act like it. When asked, she would tell people she was "sixty-five plus," and that was the end of that discussion.

Then one day, a couple of years into her diagnosis, she went to the hospital for what she thought was a simple procedure. However, the cancer had spread quickly since her last appointment. Not only would she not return home, but she was intubated and was never to speak again.

As I sat by her side in her hospital room, I awakened to the sadness that the time for conversation had passed, especially the time for questions and answers. But I did have questions, questions that I had never asked but wished I had, questions about the details of stories I wished I would have better committed to memory so as to pass them on more perfectly. But now, she couldn't answer me. If only I had written them down or taken a more serious interest when she had been in a mood to share.

The stories of our family and our faith are crucial in shaping the lives of our children and grandchildren, but this effect can extend to many others who may have the blessed opportunity of hearing or reading them as well. Everyone's history is ripe with such stories, but if we don't write them down, then they are sure to be forgotten. The details can be wiped away over the movement of time and the fading of memories.

Jesus told stories, so they *must* be important. It was the method He used to reach out to the people He came to save. His stories were most often parables, simple stories that teach a moral lesson. Some of His most well-known—and several of my favorite—stories are those of the Prodigal Son, the Good Samaritan, the Master of the Vineyard, and the Good Shepherd, who leaves the ninety-nine to go in search of the one who was lost.

These stories of Our Lord are so *simple*, yet they deliver truth with a driving force to move and make change. I believe this is what we, as complicated people, need more than anything else. This is how it is in the lives of the saints as well. Their lives were often complex and sometimes testaments of great suffering, but their stories deliver the same Gospel simplicity that a life in Christ is the only way. Their stories inspire and encourage me. If they can do it, so can I.

In his Gospel, St. Matthew shares many of the stories he must have heard firsthand from Jesus. And he wrote them down so others might hear or read them too, even telling his own story of being called: "As Jesus passed on from there, he saw a man named Matthew sitting at the customs post. He said to him, 'Follow me.' And he got up and followed him" (Matt. 9:9). Simple but effective. Matthew listened and obeyed. I'm sure his wasn't an easy journey of following Jesus, but he stuck with it, and God took care of the rest.

So it is with us; so it is with me. If we just listen, and follow, and stick with it, God will help us see it through. I've read and been told often that we are "called to be saints." They are our models to imitate, and, like St. Matthew, they followed Christ and modeled Him for us. I believe that a part of this journey home is that we are also called to share our lives and what Jesus has done for us, also like St. Matthew.

These are the "books" that Jesus is writing in us and through us. Truth is important, but truth through story and personal testimony is power. We can and should share our stories with others, especially of what God has done for us, because, perhaps, they will be the help and encouragement they need.

I am not so sure that this was my intention when I decided to journal an account of each day of our adoption process. We carefully conserved every correspondence, conversation, and day's thoughts to help us remember what we had done, what had been said, and how we felt about all that we were encountering. Little did I know when I set out that what would come from these scribblings and clippings would be an account of a turbulent time in which God would use trials and joys, both of immense size, to seek and save the lost in more ways than one.

I can remember telling someone long ago that if I could not have children, I would adopt. However, I also remember telling someone that I would *never* go to Russia. Though the details of these conversations escape me now, for whatever reason, God imprinted these two statements on my soul, and something had to give.

Anyone who grew up during the Cold War will understand why that was a country definitely *not* on my bucket list. That place, as the heart of the USSR, had frightened the world, and most certainly it had frightened *me*. For decades, they were more than just competition in the space race, they were *the bad guy* stationed and looming behind the Iron Curtain (a disturbing term if there ever was one, especially in the imagination of a child!).

They were the enemy. There had been the Korean and Vietnam Wars, the Cuban Missile Crisis and countless bomb scares, and the Berlin Wall and Airlift, just to name a few of the most memorable events of the Cold War. And though many of those things happened before I was born or when I was a little girl, my memories of them are laced with sadness. I knew many who spoke so poorly about these events, which didn't help very much, but the aura that hovered over these decades was much more than disgust, shame, or sadness—it was *fear*. As a homebody born with a cautious character, keeping a place like that at arm's length (or hopefully a little farther) was top priority.

The story that *I* wish to share, however, is about adoption. A story, in more ways than one, about trust conquering fear, a story about letting go but never giving up. A story of relentless pursuit. What I mean to say is that while this story may be about a little boy in a scary place and the mother that is after him, it is much more than that. As St. Paul put it, "But when the fullness of time had come, God sent his Son, born of a woman, born under the law, to ransom those under the law, so that we might receive adoption" (Gal. 4:4–5).

What I have had to learn, and what each of us must take to heart, is that being an adopted son or daughter of God is not a one-time, passing event. It's not just a "thing" that happens at Baptism. The strongest and deepest essence of adoption is not about humans adopting humans, but God adopting humans.

Like a mother after her son, God is after us. God was after *me*. He prompts us through the Holy Spirit, and it is up to us to respond or not. These are His invitations, but we can miss out on the blessings that God wishes to give if we are not open or aware of His will for our lives.

This is especially true when life seems impossible and we feel lost or forgotten. In other words, it is when we feel orphaned and abandoned that we are less in tune than we should be to the movements of God, but it is then that He holds us the closest out of Fatherly love and is working all things out for our greater good. This is at the heart of the gospel message and at the heart of my story.

A few years after my mother passed, my husband and I made the decision to move to a smaller home. Determined to downsize and declutter, I was ruthlessly purging our belongings as we prepared for this pretty big change. On one particular afternoon during this grueling process, I peered under our bed and found yet another dusty box pushed against the wall. Reaching deep, I pulled it out, adding it to the growing collection gathering in our bedroom.

I lifted the box's lid and sifted through the childhood belongings of my now-grown children: sports pictures, yearbooks, scrapbooks, and other keepsakes. Then I saw it: a small duffle bag with the name *SASHA* embroidered on top. Gently, I lifted it out and peered inside.

There they were.

I sank into the oriental rug on the bedroom floor, cradling the two tiny red shoes. I held them, worn and small and fragile, in my hands. Tears filled my eyes as I fingered the soft leather. They symbolized the reality of a little boy who had been waiting for someone to come, who hadn't had much—but did have *hope*. He was a child, like all children, who just wanted a family.

As my tears fell, the room around me faded away, and I went on a pilgrimage to my past, remembering the story of that boy, remembering my story too, and realizing that both stories are actually stories of a God Who *relentlessly* pursues us.

Yes, this is *my* story—but even more, *it is the story of God's deep and personal love for each one of us.*

I

Dreams of More

You have made us for Yourself, O Lord, and our hearts are restless until they rest in You.

—St. Augustine

As I would come to learn from a small boy in a faraway place, my two early memories of laughter are two more than many children across the world get to experience in their childhood years. One of them is of my father riding the waves at the beach on a boogie board, the other of my mother sitting on my father's lap and laughing hysterically. In both instances, the joy of the moment became infectious, gripping my sister and me. But in the space of time shortly thereafter, life in my house growing up seemed to become much more serious. It was almost like everything became difficult or problematic, even things that should have been no big deal at all.

My childhood was not unhappy, but I mean to say that it was somewhat empty. Wasn't there more joy to be had? More fullness, more laughter than what I was experiencing in the day-to-day? I thought this must be, and the single greatest determination of my childhood was that I was going to find it. My parents I now know had a difficult marriage, one that was overshadowed by the early death of their dreams and my father's undiagnosed depression—both also root causes of the stern nature of our household. Along with the somewhat rocky relationship I had with my only sister, I knew that family life, in addition to life overall, was a particular area where I wanted more.

I was baptized and raised Lutheran. We attended a little stone church with a bright red door, but my memories of the Sunday services are mostly of me daydreaming during them—of the "more" of what my life could be. What any preacher said or any Scriptures that were read went in one ear and out the other. I remember the railing where we knelt down to receive grape juice once a month in small, delicate glasses and the little *click* as we placed them back into the notches on a wooden holder. I remember disliking those Sundays because the church service was long.

Did I have any kind of relationship with God at that time to sustain me through childhood? I'm not sure, but I do know that God was not a part of our everyday lives. I never really thought much about Him. In addition to my baptism, I was confirmed in a Lutheran service as well, but these seemed to be just ceremonies, like "checkmarks" on the list of activities I was required to accomplish during my growing-up years.

So, there were a lot of dreams in my young world—dreams of my own future, my own children, and how I would raise them. Dreams of joy and a husband with a smile who would find me and take me away to a life of adventure, dreams of children chasing dogs through the backyard, dreams of family dinners and talk of that day's highs and lows, and dreams of camping in the backyard. Needless to say, I was determined that there would be more laughter and more joy in my home than I had experienced.

One of the few times my stoic, formal father intervened in my life was to insist that I attend Auburn University. He liked this university because there were "rules," such as curfews and "dorm mothers" for all the students, men and women alike. When I questioned him about going there, he said that I could go anywhere I wanted—but he would only pay for Auburn.

It was actually at Auburn that the Christian faith I had been gifted with at my baptism began to wake up. Right away I attended church with friends, but I was intimidated because they always dressed in stylish outfits, and it was hard for me to compete with them. In fact, I actually made some of my own clothes because I didn't have the money to buy a wardrobe. Unfortunately, church at times felt more like a social or a competition than a place to worship.

During my freshman year, I also joined a sorority, and it was there, of all places, that I encountered God, perhaps for the first real time in my life. In my sorority chapter room, a young woman came to speak to us about Jesus. At the end of her talk, she passed around a basket and offered to pray with anyone who wrote their name on a piece of paper and placed it inside.

I knew I needed help. I longed for acceptance, love, and a way of life that was more than what I was experiencing and had experienced. I wanted something—or someone—greater that would bind me together in this adventure of life. In hindsight, I'm positive God was nudging me—longing to fulfill the greatest desires of my heart, the *more* that I had been so desperate for. So, I took the young woman up on her offer, on the lifeline she had extended, and placed my name in the basket.

A few days later, we were to meet in the main gathering place at Auburn, the bustling War Eagle Cafeteria. Crowds of hungry college students filtered in and out. Some were focused on sitting still, leaning over a textbook to cram for an afternoon exam, but some groups were more there for a good time with friends, laughing loudly and telling jokes over hamburgers and fries. I was more nervous than hungry and shuffled through the maze of chairs to a table tucked away in a corner where I met the young woman.

She invited me to pray, so I did. I asked God to come into my heart and my life. It was simple and sweet, but effective. I had been to church every Sunday and gone through all the Christian motions, but I consciously opened my heart to the Lord, truly, for the first time. My new friend assured me that I was now "born again" and that God's Spirit was now guiding my life.

I didn't grow a halo or speak in tongues, but there was a particular way that the Spirit was leading me, for sure, although I could not have articulated it at the time. And "it" happened rather quickly: his name was Jack.

I met Jack when he arrived at Auburn as a junior. I was a sophomore and was going through Little Sister Rush to his fraternity, a process to become a "little sister" to him and his brothers. He had been asked to pick me up and bring me to a social to meet the brothers. Because he had been given a picture of me, he knew what I looked like and even recognized that we had had a class together. As I came down the stairs of my dorm and through the door into the lobby, Jack was leaning against the counter waiting for me.

There was something about him, something new, something different. He carried a smile rooted in something I didn't have. What I remember most, however, was knowing instantly that he was meant *for me*. In retrospect, was I able to see into his heart as well? Did God speak to me in that moment and open my eyes to love? I don't know. But later that evening back in my dorm room, I called my mother and told her I had met the man I was going to marry. Years later, I would feel similarly about my son as well. I knew without question that God had destined him *for me*.

As we spent more and more time together, I witnessed in Jack and his friends a different way of attending church, since they were Catholic. Growing up, we learned that Catholics were at best ignorant and at worst teaching a false kind of Christianity, but my experience through Jack was radically different. His parents were devoted to their family and to their Faith. Unlike my experience, religion was not just a Sunday affair; the faith was *lived*. Jack and his six siblings remember their father inviting each of them to join him for daily Mass, and Jack grew up with a devotion to the Holy Eucharist and to Our Lady, who was also loved by his mom, Bernadette (called Chubby, a childhood nickname).

Often, on a Sunday, Jack and I would be with his friends, and all of a sudden one of them would blurt out, "We have to go to Mass!" A bit of chaos would ensue as they scrambled to tidy themselves up and find a ride to make it to church on time.

It struck me that what they were wearing or who they might run into was not important. What mattered was that they made it to church on Sunday. After attending Mass with them that first time, I began to understand why it was so important.

Everyone went forward to receive Holy Communion, which in my Lutheran church was just a memorial, a remembrance of Jesus. Since I was not Catholic, I remained in the pew and watched Jack and his friends receive something that I could not. Their genuine reverence told me that there was something going on here beyond merely checking boxes. There was no goofing off in the Communion line; this was something to be taken seriously.

Jack approached the priest slowly and solemnly, and he genuflected just long enough to show reverence without holding up those behind him. He raised his hands high to receive what they called the Eucharist. After making the sign of the cross, he came back to pray. In that pew he was next to me, yes, but he was not *with me*. He was with Jesus, experiencing something *more*. I felt and knew that I was missing out on something—something that I knew I needed.

Jack and I were married shortly after his graduation in 1981. The following year, Jack's father and a few other franchisees purchased Krispy Kreme Doughnut Corporation, putting the company in the hands of those who knew the product and had invested their lives in the brand.

It was twenty-eight years earlier in February of 1953 when Jack's dad, Joe, opened his first Krispy Kreme doughnut shop in Mobile, Alabama. His dad hand-cut the doughnuts, placed them in a wooden proof box, then hand-fried them and glazed them. His dad would often say, "It took me three and a half years to go broke."

But when he changed locations three years later, he couldn't keep up with the demand. His success continued, with Jack working long hours in his dad's growing chain of doughnut stores.

Now, as a part of the sale agreement, Jack's father became the chairman, CEO, and president of Krispy Kreme. This was a dream come true for him, as well as quite a challenge at this stage of his life. It was hard for Joe to leave his home in Mobile for North Carolina after fifty-seven years of stability in the congenial city on the Gulf Coast, but his entrepreneurial spirit was ready and willing to help Krispy Kreme not just to stay on track, but to grow into America's doughnut.

Jack's father asked us if we were interested in moving to North Carolina with him and Jack's mom and help him accomplish his new task. Jack and I were excited at the opportunity. We looked forward to living and working in Winston-Salem and starting our lives as a married couple. As we settled into our little house, I delighted in creating a home for the two of us.

I was also looking forward to joining the Catholic Church. However, all dreams take time. Jack and I first needed to establish ourselves at a parish, and I needed to participate in RCIA, the Rite of Christian Initiation of Adults, the process of being received into the Catholic Church. God led us to Holy Family Church in Clemmons, North Carolina, where I became Catholic and celebrated my first Eucharistic meal in a community full of hospitality and welcome.

I was also eager to start a family and model it on what I always dreamed a family could be in the imaginings of my youth. We were blessed with two children rather quickly. Our first daughter, Lauren, was born in 1985, followed by our daughter Jennifer in 1987. There was a miscarriage in between, so we also have one child in Heaven. However, as Jennifer grew into a toddler and beyond, the stirrings of childhood dreams in my restless heart would *not* settle. Instead, the familiar ache for more, even despite the busyness of our lives, began to resurface.

2

On a Roller Coaster

The Lord *gave and the* Lord *has taken away.*

—Job 1:21

Jack was rising through the ranks of Krispy Kreme. As the head of brand and concept development, he had many big projects in the works, requiring much of his time and extensive travel. Jack didn't like to be away from home—but there were many meetings to attend and stores to be built, both of which took big chunks of time. I filled in as best I could with the most cheerful attitude I could muster. With my husband wrapped up in his work, perhaps I grew a tad jealous and longed to be busier too. Still, I watched the business grow with gratitude.

During this time, Krispy Kreme was in the process of shifting its focus from wholesale distribution to retail stores. After several years of developing a strategy for a new era of growth, Jack and his older brother, Mac, were beginning to put the plan into place.

The store layout realigned to focus on customers coming in the front door. Doughnut manufacturing became much more of a feature in the store design. There were many accomplishments brought about by many great people working together, including the opening of some new stores outside of their existing territory.

But what happened next, as these new stores began opening across the country, was, to say the least, *unexpected.*

Krispy Kreme opened its first store outside of the southeastern United States, in Indianapolis. This was a defining moment for the company because it showed that the new retail concept could prosper in new markets. Jack was there when the double drive-through location opened to great success. In fact, a local Indianapolis morning show host came with his sidekick, a dog named Barney. The host asked if Krispy Kreme would give the second dozen free if anyone mentioned his dog, and chaos ensued, backing up traffic on the interstate. What a commotion!

Back at the station, the news anchors said that they wanted their doughnuts too. So Jack loaded up ten dozen boxes and headed to the studio. He gave a box to the first security guard, a second box to another, and then found himself on air holding the remaining boxes of Krispy Kreme doughnuts. That morning, he became a television celebrity! This was one of the moments where Jack discovered the absolute "power of the doughnut," which we learned could be harnessed when necessary.

But it wasn't only Indianapolis. In each new city, automobiles would back up for miles for the doughnut. A news helicopter that was assigned to report on the traffic ended up landing in a nearby parking lot to get a taste. Jack discovered that boxes of doughnuts were enough to get television and radio airtime across the country, even on national television, such as *The Today Show* and *The Rosie O'Donnell Show.* Free product placement was the norm, as television shows like *Friends* and *ER* would feature the doughnuts on the show without a cost to Krispy Kreme.

But there was much going on outside of Krispy Kreme as well. Our lovely daughters were growing up quickly and were active at St. Leo Catholic School. I regularly helped out at the school, and Jack, busy as he was, served on the parish council and the school board.

As my thirtieth birthday came and went, however, the desire for another child was beginning to grow in my heart. Having grown up in a family of two girls, and now having two daughters of my own, the thought of raising a family a bit different from what I came from became important to me. Actually, the longing to change the dynamics of my immediate family and have a third child became *intense.*

Maybe this was it, a sign from God or the Holy Spirit. Was there something that God wanted me to do? Even better, was there something He wanted to do *for me?* Was He trying to *give* me the "more" I had always been searching for: more joy, more challenge, more life? Those years of childhood dreaming were flooding to the surface, being made manifest. This was the time, the opportunity, to make things different.

As we began trying to have another child, I soon discovered that it was not as easy to become pregnant as it had been before. Although I tried not to think about it, I couldn't help but worry. After several months of trying and agonizing, we went to see doctors for help.

The doctors examined us, conducted some tests, and assured us we were fine; we just needed to be patient. But I did not believe them. I had the sense or intuition that something was wrong. After two "easy" pregnancies, why were we having difficulty now? Jack and I discussed many possible causes, recalling the different issues others had faced or that we had read about. Jack's mom reminded us that he had the mumps at seventeen, and we speculated that maybe that was causing some problems now.

In the spring of 1993, an infertility specialist at Baptist Hospital in Winston-Salem agreed to see me, and he began his investigation into what the issue might be. After telling him about Jack's mumps as a teenager, he wanted Jack to be checked out as well.

After a few difficult days of waiting for the results of the tests, the call from the infertility specialist that I had been waiting for—dreading, actually—finally came. As I sat on the edge of my bed, gripping the phone, he confirmed my concerns.

"Mrs. McAleer, I'm sorry to tell you that the tests we completed on you and your husband reveal that the likelihood of you conceiving a child are extremely low."

My heart and my hope shattered as I listened to him tell me that we would probably never be able to conceive a child again, though it was not entirely clear why.

"Your children are miracle children," my doctor informed me. He went on, "You really only have two options to choose from: you can get off this roller coaster and be grateful for the two children you have, or we can begin costly fertility procedures for which I cannot guarantee success."

With the most positive voice I could muster, I thanked him for his help and advice and hung up the phone.

After the call ended, I sat sobbing on my bedroom floor. I felt like God had slammed the door on the "more" I wanted and needed and dreamed of for so long. I knew that everything God did was for a reason, that there was some bigger plan being carried out, but that was little consolation. My five-year-old daughter

Jennifer, who was looking for me, came into the room. She put her little arms around me, and she tried to console her mother, who just needed to grieve.

I knew that I was indeed blessed to have two children—precious gifts from God. I knew that all children were "miracle children." About those things, the doctor was right.

But infertility, even secondary infertility, is a form of death that still needs to be grieved, for no desire equals that of having a child.

Infertility has been described as a death of dreams and desires—even if one experiences it later in life or if one already has children. Since the ache and call for another child and more life still beckoned, I was not willing to simply accept this kind of death. *I am a good mother,* I thought. *How could He take away the very thing for which my heart was created?*

After some reflection and discernment, Jack and I decided to forego any fertility procedures—mainly because we had already been blessed with two babies, who were now two beautiful young girls, and we were extremely grateful for them. Yet despite the door of having more biological children being closed in my face, I still felt a deep longing for another child, a longing that only seemed to increase with each passing day.

The Bible is full of stories of women and men desiring, praying for, and being blessed with the gift of a child. Through the miracle of children, parents are able to "taste" eternity and participate in the creative work of God.

Of the women I had read about in Scripture, some of my favorites were those who grieved for a child, like Hannah in the first book of Samuel. Hannah, the wife of Elkanah, longs for a child. Elkanah asks her, "Am I not better for you than ten sons?"

(1 Sam. 1:8). But Hannah was not satisfied with that, so she brought her desires before the Lord.

In her "bitterness"—what I would classify as her desperation and desire—she prayed to God through silent lips as tears streamed down her cheeks. More than that, she *begged* for a child from the maternal depths of her heart. The priest Eli thought that Hannah was drunk because she was praying so fervently. Hannah defended herself, however, explaining that she was pouring out her troubles. Eli then blessed her, saying, "Go in peace, and may the God of Israel grant you what you have requested" (1 Sam. 1:17). A short time later, the Lord remembered her pleas and gave her a child.

Couldn't God do the same for me?

Like Hannah, I grieved for another child. I would take long walks with our dog, Sam, and I would rant and rave at God. Like Hannah, I, too, probably looked as if I were drunk to those passing by as I waved my arms up at God, asking, "Why me?"

I was a new Catholic, and I didn't really know how to pray. I didn't really know the Rosary or how to ask the saints for help. I would just say things to God from my heart, as I shook my fist and looked up at the sky. I would remind him that Jack and I had married and started our family as young adults, and we were younger than most of our friends who were still growing their families.

What was so special about them? I wondered.

Weren't we good parents who enjoyed being with their children? Didn't we teach them values and raise them in the Faith?

Why wouldn't God entrust us with more children? Aren't miracles for God an easy thing to do? Why not me? Why not now?

I found it very difficult to be around pregnant women. I wondered what I looked like as I visited with them or learned of their good news. I would wonder, *Did my face betray my feelings?* Although I never heard from anyone that I didn't handle myself well, I found myself avoiding anyone who was pregnant, mainly because it was just too emotionally difficult.

Although I knew that the Lord was with me in a general kind of way—after all, I had asked Him into my life and had become a member of His Church—I believe He began to take on a more active role in my life. Or, more likely in my desperation, I began to *need* Him in a way I hadn't before.

As time passed and my worries and emotions were poured out, my heart became quieted. Maybe I was just looking for a sign, but I began to actively listen to Him, perhaps for the first time in my life. This didn't change my hopes or focus—I still wanted to be a new mother again—but I learned that God can speak to us through others as much as He can directly.

3

Leap of Faith

For I know well the plans I have in mind for you—oracle of the LORD*—plans for your welfare and not for woe, so as to give you a future of hope.*

—Jeremiah 29:11

In January of 1994, I hosted a children's clothing show in my home. It was an ordinary winter day, a day to keep busy and create a good reason to mingle and visit with other moms. A woman who introduced herself as Dee Dee came to shop, and she spoke happily about the child she was shopping for, a little girl she had adopted from Romania.

As you might imagine, I was fascinated.

Although I was doing my best to carry out my task of showing and selling clothes, I found myself showering her with questions: Who helped you do this? What is the process like? How long does it take? She spoke of adoption agencies and foreign contacts, and she was relieved to be on this side of all of the forms to fill out, phone calls to make, and government agencies to work with hand in hand. The more she answered my questions, however, the more overwhelming and impossible the whole experience sounded.

How on earth could I ever do something like this? I thought.

I tried to be a good hostess, welcoming my friends and pouring coffee, but my mind was somewhere else. I was jumping forward to all the meetings, conversations, and travel to a foreign country that would be required, not to mention the faith and courage needed to see it through.

However, despite the obvious hurdles in the way, the familiar desire for *more* refused to be squashed. In this brief but momentous encounter, I once again sensed my life was changing; God was cracking open a door to another world that I had never heard of before.

What was God thinking?

Then, as if in answer to my many questions and doubts, the *Catholic News & Herald*, our local diocesan newspaper, arrived in the mail that same afternoon. On the front page was a feature article about a new program that was being offered by Catholic Social Services on Russian adoption.

The article described a beautiful little Russian boy and his new American mother, and the story of how her maternal heartstrings were pulled to adopt. When she laid eyes on a photograph of a malnourished boy with glistening blond hair from the former Soviet Union, she knew he was her son. While the article featured photographs of the happy boy and his new mother, beneath the article was an image from a Russian orphanage of three babies in their cribs waiting to be adopted.

The article also provided contact information to inquire about the adoption program. If conceiving a third child was impossible, then maybe *this* was possible.

Later that evening, it was time to share with Jack about my rendezvous with Dee Dee, the article in the *Catholic News & Herald*, and all the thoughts and desires surfacing as a result. He knew something was up with me, that there was something on my mind. I was nervous to pull him into my idea. What if I was wrong about this? What if he thought it was a bad idea? Finally we found some time away from the girls, and I poured my heart out to him.

Jack put his hand on mine, and he listened intently to all I had to say. By the time I was done, there were hints of tears in his eyes, and he wore a small smile that told me he heard me from a place of love. Like his dad, Jack was always open to an abundance of life. He came from a large family, and his faith was strong—stronger and more courageous than mine—so of course he was open to adopting a child!

He was excited at the prospect of adoption. But he was also very busy at work, so he left this amazing opportunity in my hands.

I contacted Catholic Social Services first thing the next morning and learned that there was to be an informational meeting in Hickory, North Carolina, in April to discuss the Russian adoption program. Since the process was so new, they had no application for international adoption, so they sent me an application for general adoption.

If I wanted to begin this process, I needed to bring this application and the $400 application fee to the meeting in Hickory.

As Jack and I shared our plans with our families, we were met with both excitement and questions—but also some argument. Though Jack's mom and dad asked a few questions, they gave us their full support and said they welcomed the possibility of a new grandchild.

My parents, on the other hand, encouraged us to be grateful for our two daughters and forget such a crazy scheme. They were fearful of the possible illnesses, diseases, and problems a child "like that" would have.

But as I reflected on their words, I thought, *Isn't that the same with any child?*

Though my parents had doubts and reservations, my sister, Georgett, was interested in learning about the process, and she traveled up from Atlanta to attend the meeting in Hickory with me. Jack stayed home with Lauren and Jennifer, who were then six and nine.

Just after lunch that Saturday, we headed out to the Catholic Conference Center in Hickory. Because the drive was a little over an hour, Georgett and I had time to talk about all we might hear and see.

Though unmarried, Georgett had an adventurous and caring spirit and was interested in hearing more about the children. I, too, was excited, but I was also anxious. I had so many fundamental questions that needed answers, like cost, time frames, the health of the children, and even *what was Russia really like?*

When we arrived, I was surprised to see the large number of people in attendance. We took our seats, and one speaker after another addressed the gathering. There was Catherine Winfree from Catholic Social Services (CSS), then Rita, who was the Russian representative for CSS, and finally Ludmilla, who, as the director of child rights, was responsible for nearly all of the orphanages in Russia.

What they had to share with us about Russia and its orphans was heart wrenching. I listened intently as they explained what had happened in Russia after the Soviet Union had dissolved in 1991. With a newly independent and more open Russia came a wave of entrepreneurs, as most legal barriers to business had now been removed. It seemed that fortunes could now be made by many who had been oppressed for so long. But, while the people of Russia enjoyed many new freedoms, there was rising economic and political instability during this period, and their future seemed uncertain.

Wanting to be honest about the situation, the speakers revealed that this was a time of turmoil in Moscow. If we wanted to continue with the process, we would be heading into a turbulent situation in Russia, for its people and especially its orphans. Due to the economic uncertainty of the time, the early nineties saw an influx of children into Russian orphanages. By 1994, there were approximately three hundred thousand children in the orphanage system. But they were the lucky ones. Reports also indicated about four times that number of homeless youth wandering the streets.

The majority of the children living in orphanages were "social orphans," which meant that one or both of their birth parents were still alive. These children had been handed over to the state for any number of reasons, including poverty, the drug or alcohol addiction of a parent, or a physical disability of the child. At eighteen, the children in Russian orphanages were turned out to fend for themselves. Although they might receive some government assistance, their future was not very bright or filled with hope.

Although the CSS representatives and their Russian contacts did their best to frame the situation as positively as they could, they were honest. The underlying message was that life in a Russian orphanage was less than ideal. In all likelihood, many of these children would suffer from malnutrition, emotional trauma, and any number of undiagnosed or misdiagnosed illnesses. While these children were routine oriented and patient, they would have rarely, if ever, been outside the orphanage grounds.

But, like all children, they desperately needed and longed for homes and families, for someone to hold them and love them.

I felt the anxiety receding and the sadness of my infertility being replaced with hope. Like the once-infertile mother of Samson, who received a visit from an angel to proclaim to her the hope of a son, a new trust for the future was welling up. My heart was being opened too, and I felt a bit intoxicated about the possibility of a new child coming into our family in a rather unconventional way—through *international adoption.*

Unsurprisingly, we learned that it was more difficult to adopt a baby from Russia than an older child. Babies were easier to place with couples, as they would likely have less issues or "baggage." The older a child was, the easier it was for him or her to be adopted. Both Georgett and I sensed that though the Russians were struggling with giving up their children, they also recognized that these children desperately needed loving homes.

Following the presentations, we mingled, and Georgett and I were both tantalized by the many pictures of adorable children who were waiting in orphanages to be adopted: sweet little girls in simple dresses, handsome boys with simple smiles, all of them in need of a mother.

I had the opportunity to meet a sweet child, Lonia, who had recently been adopted from Russia. As I visited with Lonia's mom, Margaret Heatherly, I was in awe that she had actually gone through this challenging process and had emerged from it with this beautiful son. She was very encouraging, but she was also honest about her experience.

As she discussed the many different possibilities and scenarios that the children may be facing, such as underdevelopment and fetal alcohol syndrome, I began to feel overwhelmed again. Margaret must have sensed the anxiety, or perhaps, observed my concern through my facial expressions because she quickly and emphatically reassured me that the children were beautiful and loving, and her son was a living example of this.

That day I took a leap of faith and handed in our application and fee. Our adoption process had officially begun.

One might think that throughout this meeting I would be tempted to run, to continue on with life as I had grown to know it. However, my resolve and determination had only grown from the time I stepped into the room. Just as I knew that Jack was the right man for me, I knew that this was the right path for our family to take.

I wasn't about to turn my back on God's plan, especially now that He was hinting at what it might be, though it was still very cloudy and unclear, and I was still *very* apprehensive.

Later that same evening after the girls were asleep, I found myself alone in my room. I sat alone on the edge of my bed in the quiet and questioned what I had done that day. It still didn't make sense—what God had done to me, what God was doing now. Rummaging through some of the prayer cards that I kept in the drawer next to my bed, I came across one a dear friend had given me.

> For I know well the plans I have in mind for you, says the LORD, plans for your welfare, not for woe! plans to give you a future full of hope.
>
> When you call me, when you go to pray to me, I will listen to you.
>
> When you look for me, you will find me.
>
> (see Jer. 29:11–13)

Though the Lord was still in the process of revealing His plan to me, a part of me was excited to be on the ground floor of something really big: the excitement of another child and the blessing of giving a new life to a child in need.

4

The Home Study

Bring back my sons from afar, and my daughters from the ends of the earth.

—Isaiah 43:6

Two months had passed since the meeting in Hickory; it was now June of 1994. I met with our social worker, Marie Givner, from Catholic Social Services, and she was lovely, both inside and out. Marie looked to be about my age, with pretty, dark brown hair, and she had a family similar to mine.

We discussed what was presented at the meeting in Hickory, as well as what would be involved in our "home study." This was the first step in the adoption process, in which Marie would assess our skills as parents. Our home study would begin after approval from the state of North Carolina, and it would include both joint and individual interviews, as well as home visits. She forewarned me it would take two to four months.

I was a bit nervous about this; I thought we were good parents, but others might see things differently.

I remember when Marie came to our home for the first time. As she looked around, I wondered what she was thinking. I liked to decorate with bright colors, and I hoped she did too. I'm sure I whispered a silent prayer that she could see and sense the love that lived there.

During the home study, we were asked to be specific about the age of the child we were interested in and the medical conditions we were willing to accept. Marie assured me that most of the medical information on the children was fairly accurate, but there just wasn't much of it. In Russia, children had to either be emotionally disturbed or deemed medically "unacceptable" to be adopted, and you never really knew just how ill a child truly was (if at all). However, it was probable that most of the children were underweight and undersized and looked and behaved younger than they actually were—likely due to a lack of care and attention.

Marie said that the adoption process was about nine months from start to finish—just like a normal pregnancy! Once a child had been identified for us, we would be asked to send pictures so the child could know about us—about his or her new family. Based on her experience, Marie assured me that most of the children were able to bond well with their new families.

Despite the sheer number of hoops we would need to jump through before actually traveling to Russia, we discussed what the trip might look like. Husbands and wives were encouraged to go together, and I was excited to learn it *was* possible to bring your children as well.

I knew that was what I wanted.

One might ask why I would want to bring my young children to a country so affected by conflict and poverty, a place I had declared I would never go myself. But I knew in my heart that we needed to do this together as a family, and our daughters needed to share in every aspect of this adventure. Sometime early in this process, Jack and I shared with the girls our plans and hopes. Lauren, being nine, had a greater understanding of what it could mean to have a new sibling and was excited about the possibility. Jennifer, as a six-year-old who mimicked her older sister's cues, followed suit and was giddy at the idea.

Though I was eager to get started (and the girls were eager for this idea we had shared with them to become reality), it also sounded like there would be a lot of "hurry up and wait" in this adoption journey—starting now.

A few weeks later, I sat in my living room waiting for Marie, who was coming over to discuss the next steps in the adoption process. I stared out the window and admired our street. We lived in a beautiful neighborhood, with little traffic and lots of trees. Before long, their leaves would transform into a beautiful array of reds and golds before the first snowfall would cover what was left of them. That day, however, it was hot and sunny—though not humid—and children of all ages played up and down the street. As I watched, I couldn't help hoping that one day there would be one more child out there climbing the trees, kicking a ball, or riding a shiny new bike. My heart stirred with anticipation.

Our house, however, needed a bit of work. As I waited, my eyes darted about the room, making a mental note of everything I wanted to get done before the home visit. Jack and I loved "fixer uppers," and this house definitely fell into that category. We liked remodeling and enjoyed doing some of the work ourselves; however, this project would require some expert help.

Marie's knock brought me back to the present. Sam barked like mad, as usual, and as I answered the door, I relaxed immediately. Though we had met only a couple of times in person, Marie and I had become fast friends. I loved how she was reassuring and calm but also knowledgeable and concrete.

Marie suggested we go ahead and call the U.S. Immigration and Naturalization Service (INS) office in Charlotte and ask for form I-600A. Wow, now that sounded intimidating! I felt my anxiety kicking in.

Again, I wondered, *What have we gotten ourselves into?*

I was reminded of the book I loved as a child, *A Wrinkle in Time* by Madeleine L'Engle, in which the characters of Meg and Charles brave a dangerous journey to find their father and bring him home. Jack and I were making plans to travel to a strange land to find and bring home our child.

With all the uncertainty, I was grateful to have something concrete to accomplish.

However, the conversation turned to me and my story, my upbringing, my parents, my memories. This seemed a lot like therapy, and, as I shared some of my history with her, I learned more about myself and my emotional state and felt secure in the decisions I had made to get to this point.

During this point in my life's journey, I didn't fully comprehend the depth of my baggage and where it came from. I just knew the general issues that I struggled with. It would be years later when Fr. Dave Pivonka sat and prayed with Jack and me that I would recognize the particular "spirits" that always seemed to trip me up and cause me great pain—and why they did. For now, all I could share with Marie was that I was raised to be "perfect," to not make mistakes, which is actually impossible. Only God is perfect. Striving for perfection can lead to other things—like guilt (for not being perfect) and despair (when you realize that you are *not and never will be* perfect).

Marie and I also discussed Jack and me as a couple, how we complemented each other, how we helped each other, and how our different childhood experiences had formed us into who we were. I laughingly shared with Marie how I was the second of two girls and Jack was number six in his family of seven—though he was also the oldest of the "second set," which possibly gave him some qualities of a first child!

I couldn't even imagine growing up in a family like his. My sister and I had our own rooms, though we did share a bathroom. Jack shared almost everything. From what I could see, life in a large family helped one to be good with people, able to "go with the flow," at least more than I had experienced. It was hard to be high maintenance in a large family.

Even more of a substantial difference in our family trees came from our extended members. I grew up knowing five of my cousins from my father's side, though I had seven cousins on my mother's side who lived in California and whom I rarely ever saw. So that gave me twelve first cousins to talk about. Then there was Jack—who boasted eighty-one first cousins alone! When I would ask him about them all, he would laugh and reply that he knew *most* of their names, but he might miss a few.

As you can now imagine, holidays growing up were *very* different for Jack and for me. Christmas morning was just the four of us, opening our presents happily, but at a slow and quiet pace. My parents would invite my Great-Aunt Ellie—who was actually quite the character—to our Christmas festivities, so the five of us would sit around our dining room table and enjoy my mom's yummy lunch. Afterward, my father would entertain us with "Christmas favorites" from his favorite singer, Mario Lanza, on the stereo in our living room.

Later, after everyone else had gone off to do their own thing, I would lie down on the carpeted floor in the living room and inch my way up under our Christmas tree. By squinting my eyes, the colorful lights twinkled and glowed and reflected on all the beautiful ornaments scattered throughout the tree, causing them to shimmer and sparkle even more. "Hidden" in my secret place, I would dream of my life one day—a life filled with sparkle and excitement.

Meanwhile, a little farther south, Jack was enjoying his Christmas day chaos. After opening the multitude of presents at their home, the nine of them would pile in the car to visit both sides of the family, as the Carters and the McAleers—both boasting ten children—were all close by. Since the Carters consisted of nine girls and one boy and were pretty much teetotalers, lunch was best suited there, though there was still lots of love and laughter. The evening was reserved for the McAleer family, as that's where the Christmas "party" happened. The McAleer family had five sons and five daughters, as well as lots of love, laughter, and party punch.

It was this large, unruly, messy life—this very full life—that I desired for my family too.

Finally, Marie and I discussed how infertility is a silent grief, a monthly death of hopes and dreams, and how there is so little acknowledgment and support for the women and men who are suffering with this cross. Marie understood this cross, and she seemed to understand me.

Though I was willing to do anything to get there, I really wanted the end result. I wanted my child, and I had prayed to God not for faith but for signs. Well, here in front of me were both bundled in one person. If I was *control* and *worry*, then Marie was *trust* and *hope*, and she had promised to be with me every step of the way.

The summer of 1994 passed quickly. Before we knew it, it was the end of August. Marie called and said that Catherine Winfree had referrals on several three- and four-year-old boys. She reminded us that at age five the children were sent to a new home for older orphans. So there was a bit of a push to get these little guys out and adopted before they turned five. She said that she would get as much background information on the children as she could.

I felt my hopes rising.

However, Marie raised a new question during the call that we had not considered: would we change our child's name? Catherine had adopted a two-year-old little boy and changed his name, mainly because she believed it was important for it to sound more "American."

Now there was one more thing to think about!

A few days later, Jack and I met with Marie in person. It was time to discuss the next steps in the process so that one of these several little boys could be *our* little boy. Marie informed us that there was an adoption packet of personal items and papers that we needed to get our hands on and put together for the INS. These items included birth certificates; our marriage license; medical checks on both of us; reference letters from family members, friends, and work; and criminal background checks, not to mention form I-600A. It sounded almost like a scavenger hunt of some sort.

The easier items to lay hold of would be the reference letters from friends and family. We knew right away one person we would ask: Jack's dad. We were both pleased and touched by the letter his dad wrote for our home study:

Dear Marie Givner:

In response to your letter about the application of my son and daughter-in-law, Jack and Jamie McAleer, to adopt a child through Catholic Social Services, Mrs. McAleer and I are 100% in favor of this adoption.

I'm sure Jack and Jamie preferred to increase their family the natural way, but after several unsuccessful years, turned to the medical profession for advice. After completing their examinations, they were informed they could have no more children. We are very proud of their decision.

Mrs. McAleer and I are from families of ten children—we have seven children and eighteen grandchildren—the more the merrier. God bless you folks at Catholic Social Services for the job you do with these babies and for making a married couple's life complete.

Sincerely,
Joseph A. McAleer

On a lighter note, Marie said she would get us a list of items to bring along as gifts for the Russians we would be meeting and working with. At first, we thought this was strange—as if we would need to bribe people every step of the way just to do what was right—but she assured us that it was customary. We wouldn't have far to look for these surprises as we thought it would be fun to bring gifts from Krispy Kreme, such as tee shirts, pens, and whistles.

A week or so later, I bumped into my new friend Dee Dee. I ended up asking her many more questions about her experience adopting, but her answers only caused me frustration. She had so many stories to share—but even though her own story had a happy ending, many were discouraging. She recounted how in one situation, the medical diagnosis of the child sounded too overwhelming for the adoptive parents to take on, and in another, the correct paperwork required from the foreign government never materialized. So both adoptions crumbled.

Would mine have a happy ending? I wondered. Even after all of the research I had done and all the meetings I had been a part of, it still seemed like she knew so much, and I knew so little. I felt like she had seen the light while I still sat in darkness.

During this period, there were many days that I felt like I was stuck in a muddy swamp, trying my best to get to solid ground. This was one of those days. This woman had already adopted a child. She had gathered the paperwork, done the interviews, and had seen it through to the other side. I came away from our encounter feeling anxious and helpless.

I thought, *Maybe I should just do what so many have said—including my own parents—be happy with what I have, move on, and enjoy all that the world has to offer. Is this* really *what God wants for me? This process is so vast that I cannot even wrap my head around it. Is it even possible? Am I crazy to undertake this? Am I being courageous and strong willed or just plain foolish? Please, God, send me a sign.*

After a day or two of moping, I gathered my courage to visit U.S. Representative Steve Neal's office in Winston-Salem, which was located close to our home. Though we had no personal connection with Congressman Neal, I was in search of form I-600A, which up to now had eluded me. I had made many calls to the Charlotte INS office in an attempt to get this form in my hands, and, short of driving to Charlotte, a trip to the congressman's office in my hometown was the next step. "Let's get this done" was my maxim for this day.

When I arrived at Congressman Neal's office, I met with a nice man named Jim Phillips, an assistant to the congressman. He explained that they did not have the I-600A form on hand, but he called the INS office in Charlotte and spoke to someone there (I had only gotten a recording), requesting that an I-600A form be sent ASAP directly to him. He said he would call me as soon as it came in.

Now this was progress!

I ended up sitting and chatting with Jim for a while. He was an older man, very patient and kind, and easy to talk to. I felt like I needed to explain why I needed an I-600A form, so I shared my story.

After I was finished, he said, "So, you are going to adopt a Soviet child?" The directness of his stark question shocked me.

"Yes, I guess I am," I managed to reply.

I again thought, *Why am I doing this? I have two children already.* His question forced me to examine my motives and served to strengthen my resolve. I did wish to make a difference in a person's life, as well as enlarge my family; these were my motives, and I was firmly grounded in them.

This gentle man went on to share that he and his wife had been working in adoption and foster care for more than thirty years. He said that he would sometimes accompany his wife on her adoption placements. On one occasion, they took a seven-year-old little girl to the train at Tanglewood Park to meet her prospective adoptive parents. Jim and his wife sat on a nearby bench and watched her play on the train.

A few days later, they had another meeting, but this time the couple brought along their son, who was close to the girl's age. The children played like they had known each other their whole lives. "Can we do this again, or can I come play at your house?" the little girl asked the couple.

"Well," the mother asked, "how would you like to come and live with us at our house and be a part of our family?"

The girl's eyes lit up with excitement, and soon she became their daughter. Many years later, all grown up, she came to visit Jim and his wife, and they were amazed at just how beautiful she had become. As Jim finished his story, he said, "Isn't it wonderful what love can do?"

I was very moved and humbled by this story. Not only was it touching and beautiful, but it was unsolicited and unexpected. The more I spoke with other people about this adoption, the more evidence there seemed to be that God, in the end, would see us through.

A few days later, we received form I-600A in the mail from Congressman Neal's office. How wonderful to have service like that! Maybe our government *does* work for us, after all! And maybe—just maybe—this adoption was meant to happen.

Jack and I scrambled to gather all of the necessary forms and make the necessary visits so as to finally send off our adoption packet to the INS. As part of the process, we needed to be fingerprinted so that the FBI could do a criminal background check on us. Our local police station in Winston-Salem only fingerprinted on Thursdays from two to four in the afternoon, so we picked up Jennifer from school (Lauren had gone to a friend's house) and drove straight there.

Jennifer was fascinated as the officer took her fingers and rolled them across the ink before planting them firmly on the official paper. This was a simple procedure; it only cost five dollars for both of us (Jennifer's were free), and it only took about fifteen minutes. *Easy enough*, we thought to ourselves as the three of us left with our cards full of prints.

In late September 1994, I went to see Dr. McDowell for a physical exam, the last item I needed for our packet. This visit was mainly for my adoption medical form, but it turned out to be another form of therapy as well. While I waited for Dr. McDowell to come into the room, his nurse helped me, and we talked. After we discussed why I was there, she shared with me that she also had two children, could physically have no more, and had been considering adoption as well.

Dr. McDowell spent a lot of time talking with me. He listened to my story of infertility and was very understanding. We discussed how difficult infertility is. He agreed that it is a "silent grief." He described it as a loss, a death of dreams. He spoke of patients he had tried to help who risked all the money they had to try for a child. My heart ached for these patients of his who, like me, longed for a child. At that moment, I felt so blessed and grateful that I had two beautiful little girls to go home to, and yet I also understood the pain of his patients. There is often an immediate bond between people who share difficult experiences, such as a heart attack, cancer, loss of a loved one—and infertility.

Finally, after countless visits, calls, and digging, we had all of the packet items necessary in our possession. With Marie's blessing, we sealed them all up together, our life seemingly summarized in a handful of documents, and, along with the I-600A form, shipped them to the correct government officials.

We had done everything we had been told. Now, we simply had to rely on the recipients of these forms to do their jobs.

And wait.

5
The Call

Who may go up the mountain of the LORD*?*
Who can stand in his holy place?

—Psalm 24:3

At eight thirty on a Wednesday evening in early October, the phone rang. It was Marie Givner. We made small talk for a few moments, then she said that Catherine Winfree and a woman named Svetlana, who would be our contact in Russia, agreed that we were good candidates to adopt a child. What a beautiful compliment! What a relief! Though these were only words and opinions, which are a far cry from official or governmental approval, they were a sign of peace that we were on the right path, clearing the right hurdles at the right time.

Although our home study had not yet been completed, they had a specific child in mind for us. In our home study, we had requested a little boy, as we already were blessed with two little girls. As Providence would have it, we had already heard about a certain little boy from our friends and neighbors Beth and Chris Lyndon, who were also in the process of Russian adoption. As a result, they were familiar with several children in the orphanage.

His name was Alexander.

He was four years old. We did not yet know his birthday, but we did know he was a blond-haired, blue-eyed, happy little boy who liked to sing. Marie said that, like most of the children in the orphanage, he was small for his age. Because he struggled with the food, the doctors diagnosed him as having lactose intolerance, which meant he was eligible for international adoption. Apparently, he was a favorite with the orphanage staff, who affectionately called him Sasha, and they really wanted to see him adopted.

I was both nervous and excited, and paced back and forth across the kitchen as wonders swirled through my heart and head. *Was this our son?* What a thought! A thought I didn't think would ever enter my mind, a thought once condemned by the diagnosis of infertility. *Our son!* How could this *not* be what God wanted for us, to embrace such a child as our own? It was obvious now: This is what God wanted for us and for this little boy. This was his will for us. I could see it as clear as day.

After I hung up the phone, I sped upstairs to where our family was gathered on our bed. I told them about the phone call. Chaos ensued. Both Lauren and Jennifer started jumping up and down as if our bed was a trampoline. Jennifer was laughing and calling out his name, "Alexander!" in between jumps. Lauren, always a bit more serious, asked, "Mom, what is lactose intolerance?"

I laughed and confessed that I didn't really know. I said that whatever it was, it didn't matter—only that "it" was getting him out of Russia.

Sensing Lauren's seriousness, Jennifer quieted down a bit to express her concern about his medical problem, but then we all laughed about all the problems each of us had. Lauren thought it was funny that she and her dad would be the only brown-haired members of our family. Though she didn't say it outright, I could see that Jennifer was happy that her new little brother would look like her. I thought to myself that through the miracle of hair color, I was both a blonde—like Jennifer and Alexander—and a brunette!

The following day, I called Catherine to see if she could tell me more about Alexander, as well as about the agency that would be our contact in Russia. She told me the same information that Marie had shared, though she did fill me in about Svetlana's company, the Victoria Tourist House, which seemed to be very conscientious and careful with its placement of children. She mentioned a family, the Barkers, that had worked with them and loved the experience. Catherine also thought Alexander sounded both special and adorable, but she asked us how many other children we would like to consider before choosing one to adopt.

After our joyful family discussion the night before, Jack and I knew we did not need to consider any other "options." We didn't need more time, and we wouldn't waver. We believed this is what God wanted; it was no coincidence that we learned of him the day before and bonded over the little we knew of him. We told Catherine that we wanted to pursue adopting Alexander. She replied that she would let Svetlana know and try to get us as much information as possible.

Later that day, I called my pediatrician, who was very helpful and explained that many people have an intolerance to lactose, and there are ways to control this condition. She seemed excited for me and wished us luck. When Lauren came home from school, she announced that she had told her friends about Alexander.

"What did you share about him?" I asked as casually as I could.

"Oh, just that he might become my brother."

She was as sincere as I was hopeful. He was thousands of miles away but already loved.

A few seconds later, Sam's barking alerted me to the arrival of the mailman, who put the mail through the slot in our front door every day. As I sifted through the bills and catalogs, I saw a letter from the INS. My heart stopped as I ripped the letter open.

Would it be good news? Had our I-600A form been processed and approved so quickly?

As it turned out, no. The INS letter stated that we had neglected to include copies of our marriage certificate and proof of citizenship among the seemingly dozens of forms we had been requested to send along with the original packet. Either that, or—much more likely—they had simply lost them.

This was so frustrating—two steps forward and one back. The rest of the day was a blur of irritation as things I would usually take in stride became tainted with difficulty. This process should be simpler: I should do what I'm supposed to do, and others should do what they're supposed to do without losing our documents along the way. However, as I took a moment to try to relax that evening with a glass of wine, I opened one of the catalogs that had come in the mail. On the first page was a picture of a small wooden chair with ALEXANDER painted on it.

My heart began to beat again.

The next morning, I called Catherine to let her know that our I-600A form had been returned, asking her what we needed to do before we sent it in again. She gave me her best advice, and, with a few prayers, we went ahead and sent certified copies of our marriage license, our birth certificates, and copies of our passports to the INS via regular mail.

When Lauren came home from school, she shared that she had said three prayers for Alexander in Mass. Jennifer shared that she had prayed a prayer for him and one for our cat, Friday. How wonderful that Alexander was receiving some prayers, especially from the siblings I so longed to see him playing and bonding with.

I contemplated how trying to discern the right thing to do is often like walking in the dark with no flashlight to illuminate the way. Though Jack and I were committed to seeing this to the end, no one else seemed sure of what exactly was needed. Often, all we had to go on were the suggestions of others, from family and friends as well as the adoption professionals. Everything seemed like trial and error; we just had to keep walking, step-by-step, our patience and stamina being tested along the way.

Catherine called on October 11. She relayed that new sources said that Alexander may have celiac disease in addition to lactose intolerance. Celiac disease, which is the body's inability to assimilate gluten, is an illness I had never heard of either. Catherine suggested I talk with a gastroenterologist.

She also shared that she had faxed some questions to Svetlana on our behalf, asking for Alexander's date of birth, documented health history, height, and weight, as well as the amount of time spent in the orphanage and any information on his birth parents. She said she would get back to us as soon as she heard from Svetlana.

The following day, I called my pediatrician and told her about the new information on Alexander. She said that celiac disease was a lifelong problem that needed monitoring and maintenance of a proper diet. She also said that there was no way of knowing how serious Alexander's condition was. However, once his diet was managed and maintained, he should be just fine.

She also suggested I call a pediatric gastroenterologist to discuss the celiac disease—and anything else I was concerned about—and gave me a number to try. When I did so, the doctor was not in, nor was his nurse. I was promised that one of them would call me back on Monday. Catherine was also due to get back to us then with any new information concerning Alexander that she might have discovered.

In the meantime, we waited.

Nearly a week later, we still had not heard from the gastroenterologist my pediatrician recommended. I called Marie, who always seemed to have an answer—or at least some comforting and encouraging words. She suggested I speak with Dr. Rourk, another GI who specialized in pediatrics at Baptist Hospital. I called, and I was told he would call me back. I waited. Nothing.

The next day, I called again several times and finally spoke with a nurse. She offered me the name and number of another mother whose son has celiac disease. While I was grateful for this suggestion, I said I would still very much like to speak with the doctor. I promised her that I wouldn't take up much of his time. She said that she would ask him to call me back. Marie suggested I call Duke University, and they suggested I call the University of North Carolina. They took my name and number.

It was time to stop for today. I had reached my limit.

The next day, and again at the suggestion of Marie, I called Margaret Heatherly, who had spoken in Hickory and adopted Lonia. Actually, I called her several times and left messages at her home and at her work. I can be very tenacious when pushed. When she finally returned my calls, I missed her! Oh, the difficulty of being patient. I called her back at her home, and she finally answered. *Yes!*

As I had hoped, Margaret was a wealth of information—and she was so encouraging. I needed answers, something concrete after the lack of progress of the previous days.

She listened to me share my tale and my worries about the health of the children in the orphanages, but specifically Alexander. Margaret urged me to push for a picture of Alexander and his official medical records as well. She reassured me that there were many doctors in the United States who might be able to answer some of my questions and concerns about celiac disease and Alexander's overall health. She offered to get me some names and numbers.

Margaret also said that these children's medical records were often unreliable. In Russia, a child had to be emotionally disturbed or "unacceptable" to be adopted. Russian officials wanted them adopted internationally since most Russian families could not care for children with any kind of medical condition—and thus were extremely unlikely to adopt them. Unlike in the United States and Western Europe, Russia historically did not have a culture of adoption, so few Russians even considered it as a way to grow a family.

I had heard this before, but she had actually lived it. As it turned out, her son had none of the ailments listed on his Russian medical report, but he did have some allergies and developmental delays that were not mentioned.

On a more personal note, Margaret shared that Lonia was afraid of going to school at first. He was scared that he would have to "live" there. He was also having a hard time going to celebrations, like birthday parties, because every time a celebration had occurred at his *groupa* or orphanage, a child "disappeared." Stories like these were difficult for me to hear, but I appreciated her honesty and her friendship.

I then shared with Margaret what little we knew about Alexander's own health situation. To my joy and relief, she sounded upbeat about it all. She thought his height and weight were about right for a child his age in a Russian orphanage.

We agreed to get our families together in a few days.

As I hung up the phone, I reflected on our conversation. Her advice was so good and helpful because she had "been there" and "done that." She had descended the other side of the mountain I had yet to climb. Margaret described international adoption as a leap of faith. It was one of life's greatest risks, one that could only be accomplished with an ironclad willingness. *Please Lord*, I prayed in an exhale, *help me be brave enough to take this risk.*

A bit later, the phone rang yet again. This time it was Dr. Rourk from Baptist Hospital. Amazing—not a receptionist or even a nurse but an actual doctor! He was very kind and supportive. He said he had seen many adopted children come through his practice, and his perspective was similar to that of Margaret.

More importantly, he reiterated what I had been told many times, that most of the medical records of these children were wrong. He was the first to tell me that to diagnose celiac disease, a biopsy would have needed to be done, and he did not think the Russians could or would have done that. All this meant that, as far as his health was concerned, we were to be left in the dark until he was in our arms.

6

The Picture

But if we hope for what we do not see,
we wait with endurance.

—Romans 8:25

If I wanted your opinion, I would have asked for it! I thought this repeatedly throughout the adoption process. Nearly everyone I spoke with seemed to have a bizarre comment or a mistaken bit of information to share regarding the risk we were taking, from the absurd to the hurtful. Deep down, I knew (or hoped) they were just trying to be helpful and really weren't sure just what to say in the face of what we were doing: *traveling to Russia to adopt a child.*

Many people encouraged us to learn some basic Russian words, while others said that Moscow was rather dull. One person emphatically stated that we should *not* wear jeans in Russia, as they would "steal them off of us." I knew this was an exaggerated claim, but it was not the least bit helpful to my psyche.

Another person told me to drink only bottled (or boiled) water in Russia and to always check the seals on our bottles. We were also advised not to ask too many questions, while others warned that there frequently was no toilet paper. Now *that* was more than a bit disturbing.

The most discouraging comments, however, which did the most to diminish my courage and optimism, were along the lines of: "Be very, very careful. You don't want to take on a child that would destroy the happy home you have now."

At the time, I understood that those sharing such thoughts were trying to be protective and helpful, but children, whether they come into a family by birth or adoption, do not come with guarantees. They bring their good and not-so-good stuff with them.

But isn't that like anything in life?

On a cool November morning, I curled the phone cord nervously around my fingers as I let Catherine Winfree talk. I hoped she would answer the one question at the front of my mind without my having to ask, which would give me some much-needed relief from the stresses of the process. She told me about the Barker family, who had adopted a little girl, Michelle, from Russia with the help of Svetlana and her agency. They were the first family to use this agency, and it had gone well. She gave me their number to add to my collection.

Then, she echoed all I had heard from the medical professionals the previous day—namely that the only way to diagnose celiac disease was through a biopsy, and she couldn't imagine the Russians doing that either. She asked the status of our home study, and I proudly reported that it was now complete and in Marie's hands.

"And the picture of Alexander?" I finally asked. There was a pause.

"Oh, I'm sorry, Jamie," she replied apologetically. "I forgot!"

"Oh, it's okay," I lied after a deep, shaky inhale, obviously disappointed, but she reassured me that she would call Svetlana back and request one immediately.

It turned out I had yet another person I could trust in Pat Barker. She and her husband had adopted Michelle when she was about two years old. She was their first and only child so far and was healthy and doing well.

It was from Pat that I learned firsthand about working with Svetlana and her agency. She said Svetlana and her group were first travel agents, meaning they did a good job of handling arrangements as well as showing their clients around Moscow. Pat explained to me that following the fall of the Iron Curtain, Svetlana took a group of visitors to a Russian orphanage and quickly realized the opportunity to also assist families in adopting Russian children.

Although our conversation reassured me that Svetlana's group could be trusted, I again found myself overwhelmed by the reminder that not only did I have to figure out this adoption thing, but I would also have to go to Moscow myself and *get it done.*

Margaret made good on her promise to visit, and she brought Lonia with her. He was a darling little boy, very quiet and serious, yet his whole face lit up when he smiled. This awakened my longing to see Alexander. Margaret, who was nothing short of inspirational herself, agreed and stressed the importance of getting the so-far-elusive picture in my hands.

We spoke of how common the name Alexander is in Russia and how lucky it was that his name was common in America as well (unlike her own son's name). She said many families would jump at the chance to adopt a child like Alexander and that his difficulties sounded minor in comparison to what other issues are out there.

Then she mentioned yet another reality to consider: Alexander would arrive in America speaking only Russian. In the midst of thousands of other worries, I had somehow overlooked this simple fact. Margaret suggested that he attend an ESL school first to learn English before enrolling him at St. Leo Catholic School. But, no matter what, we wanted him at school with his two older sisters, with a tutor if necessary.

She left me with some crucial Russian words we would need to know before we went.

I sat back after she left, reflecting that despite the warnings, opinions, reservations, and doubts of others, what was at stake here was a child, and Lonia had been living proof—right here in my living room—that everything we were going through was worth it. He had played beautifully with Lauren and Jennifer. His smile, which lit up the room, and the contentment on his face, I hoped, were previews of what was to come for my own family.

There were many things in this life I felt I could live with, but the regret of not seeing this through was not one of them.

I was still waiting on Alexander's picture. The waiting was so hard! So what did I do as I waited? I pestered the people I was waiting for, of course.

I called Catherine again. No, she had not yet received the picture from Svetlana but promised to call when it came. As a result, I lingered by the phone all day, and each time it rang, I rushed to pick it up eagerly, hoping that it was Catherine calling. No such luck that day. I guess I would have to wait until Monday.

One of the blessings of my Protestant upbringing was the ingrained idea that Christians should turn to the Scriptures. So, that evening I opened my Bible looking for encouragement and guidance and read from St. Paul: "Have no anxiety at all, but in everything, by prayer and petition, with thanksgiving, make your requests known to God" (Phil. 4:6).

I had certainly made my requests known to God, but with thanksgiving and no anxiety? I was thankful, in a way, for the new spark in my heart to become a mother again through adoption. But thankful for the naysayers and the negative comments? Thankful for the hurdles and the holdups? Thankful for the government officials who lost my marriage certificate? That was different. In those things, I felt God was absent or holding us up, and my anxiety was trying to fill in the gaps.

On Saturday morning, Sam's barking once again let us know the mail had come. On the floor among the usual junk mail was a very official envelope marked with the seal of the Department of Justice: another letter from the INS.

Have no anxiety at all, I recalled, and, with a deep breath, I unsealed the envelope. However, instead of the approval I was looking for, the letter stated that the INS needed our birth certificates.

What! I thought. *How frustrating this process was! We had already sent them our birth certificates. Did they lose them?* I felt more certain than ever that they had probably lost our marriage certificate the first time around. I called and left a frustrated message on Marie's answering machine. *Why does this kind of mail always seem to come on a Saturday when no one is available to contact?*

The INS was taking on an identity of its own for us. Although it was a branch of the Department of Justice, in our minds it was quickly becoming this mean and difficult "Big Brother." We had to satisfy them constantly by jumping through hoops and standing on our heads, not to mention sending and resending lost documents. *Why were they making everything so difficult?*

Jack (as he so often did) helped me let go of my frustration and move on. He once again quoted his dad, who would very often say, "Everything's going to be all right."

And it usually was.

"Let's take a deep breath and focus on the excitement of Halloween for Lauren and Jennifer," Jack suggested in his most easygoing and positive manner.

He was right: Halloween was only two days away, and there was a lot to be done.

He immediately got busy around the house as the girls and I began to carve our pumpkins (and one for Alexander also), which was a much-loved family tradition. Deep down, I knew Jack was right: though easier said than done, I had to let go for today and trust.

On the morning of October 31, the phone rang. Jack raced over and almost ripped it off the hook. It was Catherine. Jack heard the news we had been waiting for: the picture of Alexander had just arrived at her office in Charlotte. She and Jack made plans to meet tomorrow halfway and deliver this long-awaited and coveted object to our family.

While I couldn't wait to finally glimpse Alexander, I was filled with nerves. I had hung so many hopes on this little boy; I had never met him, had never seen him, yet I loved him. Seeing him for the first time would be momentous, I knew, but I felt like I was already putting pressure on him. Could he feel it, there on the other side of the world? Was he longing to see us as we longed to see him?

Given this bit of good fortune, it seemed like a good day to place an order for more birth certificates for Jack and myself. I was promised that they would come by FedEx the following day. As soon as they arrived, I would turn around and FedEx them to the INS in Charlotte—again. I hoped these would achieve our desired results and satisfy the powers that be.

I also knew I had to wrap my head around the necessary vaccines for our family to go to Russia. I called Dr. Link, who could give us the hepatitis shots, but I missed his call. Oh well. Add it to the list—and the prayers and petitions—for tomorrow.

Early in the morning, Jack awoke, drank some coffee, and drove to meet Catherine in Statesville. The drive was about two hours round trip, but I calculated that it would take a little longer than usual that day due to heavy rain. As soon as he drove off, I began to busy myself by getting the girls out of bed and ready for school (more than difficult the day after Halloween!) and with anything else that would help the time pass by.

Jack was the first to arrive at the spot where they had agreed to meet. The rain had been torrential, with heavy bands beating down on his windshield almost the whole way. He had also passed several accidents. Jack worried that Catherine might have had difficulty driving or that traffic might have gotten backed up because of the weather, and she might not make it to meet him. He knew how disappointed we would both be if that happened.

When he spotted Catherine's car pulling in, Jack breathed a sigh of relief. Though she pulled into a parking space a few over from his car, no amount of rain could have stopped him from quickly jumping out and running toward her for no other purpose than to receive the long-awaited photo. Rolling down her window just a few inches, Catherine passed him a sealed envelope. After a brief exchange about Alexander and the excitement we were feeling, Jack thanked Catherine and hurried back to his car.

As Jack was driving home, drenched from the downpour, he was tempted to open the envelope and take a quick peek. But he thought about our journey so far, all the many ups and downs we had been through together. He realized that opening this envelope was something we should do together, each supporting the other in this very special moment.

When he finally arrived home, Jack held out the envelope with a smile on his face. I was almost too scared to open it.

This was it.

Carefully I tore the seal and pulled out a square Polaroid and studied this precious picture.

The photograph was incredible.

I found myself looking at a small face with light hair. Though the colors were muted, his eyes were bright. He looked unsure or even curious about the camera; he probably had never seen one before. The expression on his face was cute, sweet, and innocent. He was being held by a smiling, dark-haired woman. She looked to be about forty, wearing a simple white shirt, and was most likely one of the "mommas" we had heard about at the orphanage.

I wondered to myself, *What is he like—my son?* I turned to look at Jack, who was sitting beside me. He had not said anything, and I realized by the tears rolling down his cheeks that he couldn't get any words out.

Although reluctant to part with the photo for even a few hours, I allowed the girls to take the picture to school and show it to their friends and teachers. It was important for them to feel every bit a part of this experience as Jack and I did, but I was also frightened to let go of the only tangible link to my little boy. What if they lost the picture or someone damaged it?

At long last the school day was done, and I drove to pick up Lauren and Jennifer. As they spilled into the car, through their excited chatter, I gleaned that everyone at school was very excited and had something special to say about Alexander—mostly how cute he was!

That afternoon, I showed Alexander's picture to my neighbor Barbara, who was a pediatrician. She was an open and honest woman, which is why I was delighted when she said that Alexander looked very healthy. From his face shape, she thought that, perhaps, he was a premature baby, or it could have been that the angle of the camera was a bit off. To her, his eyes looked very bright—and beautiful.

She agreed that children who are adopted from other countries never seem to have exactly what their medical reports describe. Barbara told me that she had cared for several children who had been adopted internationally, and, overall, they were healthy and seemed normal like other children, though one could never know for sure ahead of time.

7

The Borders Between Us

And now, LORD, for what do I wait?
You are my only hope.

—Psalm 39:8

It was early November when Lauren, Jennifer, and I went shopping for Alexander. We bought him a sweatshirt that said, "I'm the little brother!" and a cute Pooh Bear because our family loved Winnie-the-Pooh. When we got home, we gathered a few pictures and put together a small photo album of our family. We put our names on each picture of us, including Friday and Sam—who, unfortunately, liked to chew stuffed animals. He chewed the Pooh Bear, so I had to go back and purchase another one. Once we were as satisfied with our gifts as Sam was with his new chew toy, we excitedly assembled the care package and shipped it to Svetlana. Hopefully, she would bring this to Alexander to introduce him to us—his family.

Over these long weeks, as we waited for the all clear to travel to Russia to bring home our son, I would hear his little voice calling to me during the night. He knew of us now; we were no longer just an idea or a faraway dream. He had seen us in the photographs: his parents and his sisters. He, for the first time, had at least the real hope of a mother.

Every day, with every conversation, with every glance at his photograph, I was falling more in love with him. The motherly gap in my heart that I had discovered a few years earlier began to fill up with Alexander. My heart ached that he was so far away. I was scared that something would keep us from him, that we would never be united.

I prayed to God now for strength, patience, a good outcome—and that the INS would hurry up.

A couple of weeks later, on November 18, I received a phone call from my sister, Georgett. At first, I assumed she was calling to discuss Thanksgiving plans.

I was wrong.

She had seen on the news that the doors were closing on Russian adoptions because there had been something of a scandal. American agencies were accusing the Russians of exploiting their children. In response, officials in the Russian government spoke of "swindlers" and private companies from the outside scooping up Russian children for profit. The Russians threatened to halt all American adoptions beginning on December 1.

That wasn't all. Many things happening in geopolitics were working against us as well. President Clinton was trying to negotiate long-term peace with Russia while simultaneously expanding NATO across the European continent. This didn't sit well with Yeltsin, the Russian president, who saw NATO as a threat to his country.

I was paralyzed with fear. What if we lost Alexander? All of us, especially the girls, would be crushed with devastation. Despite my early prayers for signs, I had been trusting God to see us through this process, and it seemed now that He had failed us. It was all over, and we had lost.

After two horrific hours of trying, I finally got Catherine on the phone, and, unfortunately, she echoed what Georgett had relayed to me. The only sliver of hope was that our adoption was already "in process," but we needed to continue praying.

The image that kept running through my mind was the scene from *The Sound of Music* when the Reverend Mother says, "The borders have just been closed."

Captain von Trapp replies, "Then we will go over the mountains."[1]

I heard the film's music in my head, and I felt their fear and anxiety in my own mind and heart.

In desperation, I picked up my Bible and went back to Philippians 4:6: "Have no anxiety at all, but in everything, by prayer and petition, with thanksgiving, make your requests known to God."

I prayed through these verses, or at least I tried. I know I read them—many times, which seemed to me to be the same thing. Here I was again though, retreating to prayer in a tough moment. If I only ever turned to God in desperate times, would He hear me? Was He using all of this to tell me I didn't deserve Alexander, as if He were trying to teach me a lesson? Why had He brought us this far only to have happenings on the world stage beyond our control seemingly snatch him from our arms?

Jack and I knew that the best way to get to the truth of what was really going on—and how it would affect our adoption—was to

1 Richard Rodgers et al. *The Sound of Music* (Milwaukee: Hal Leonard Corporation, 1981).

speak to someone in Russia. The only Russian contact we had was Svetlana, though we had never before spoken by phone. Since Moscow is eight hours ahead of Eastern Standard Time (EST), we called her business number at 1:15 a.m.

Twice we got through to a friend of Svetlana's. When we told her about our situation, she told us not to worry. She knew who we were, and, as far as she could tell, nothing had changed in Russia regarding international adoption. If we wanted to speak with Svetlana herself, though, we would need to call back in half an hour, she said.

So we did—at 1:45, 2:15, and again at 2:30 a.m., each time reaching Svetlana's friend. We were exhausted and needed some sleep, so we crashed for a few hours. We got up around 6 a.m. and called again. Finally, we reached Svetlana. She knew who we were, and though she also reassured us that nothing had formally changed regarding Russian adoptions, she was still concerned.

"I don't want to lose Alexander," I pleaded.

"No, you do not want to lose Sasha," Svetlana agreed. "I will call as soon as I hear anything."

When we hung up, I wanted to cry, scream, and pray, but I felt too tired and overwhelmed for any of the three. Was this a dream or a nightmare? How could I convince the INS to hurry? Where were they with our paperwork? Should I call Congressman Neal? Should I ask others to pray?

The alarm sounded a few hours later and the business of getting the girls and our family settled in for the day was a welcome distraction. With my peace slowly returning, I collected my thoughts and lined them up one by one. All I could do was carry on as if the adoption was going to happen. I knew that I needed to work on getting our shots for our potential trip overseas. I knew I needed to finish my shopping for Alexander for his arrival—*if* he arrived. I knew I was getting ready to start my period—a painful reminder of its own. Lastly, I knew I needed coffee. At 8 a.m., I would be back to the phone calls. I had promised to call Georgett back. Catherine needed to hear what Svetlana had said.

The INS needed to hear from me as well.

Lord, help me, please.

When I awoke a couple of days later on November 21, I was greeted by Lauren, Jennifer, and Jack with breakfast in bed. It was my thirty-fifth birthday, and breakfast in bed was one of our family's birthday traditions. To be awoken by a feeling other than fear and anxiety was like an oasis. It was so reassuring to be served by those whom you love and love you in return, and to know that with family you never have to face your fears and struggles alone. Although Alexander was not physically there, I carried him in my heart. Come April, I hoped, I would be serving *him* breakfast in bed.

A few days had now passed since we first heard of the escalating tensions between America and Russia, and as time does, it helped me go from panic to calm to, finally, hope.

But before I could finish my egg on toast, the phone rang.

Jim Phillips from Congressman Neal's office was calling. He had heard from his contact at the FBI that they never received our fingerprints from the INS.

What!

What was going on? Were they lost? What are we supposed to do now? Was there someone at the INS losing our marriage certificates *and* our birth certificates *and* our fingerprints on purpose, someone with an animus to adoption or Russian adoption? How could this kind of neglect be explained in any other way?

I immediately called the INS. I told the woman who answered that it was my birthday and would really appreciate some help and good news.

Unfortunately, she was able to give me neither. Meanwhile, Jim Phillips also called the INS and eventually got through to a supervisor named Tommy Thorn. Jim explained our story and where we were in this adoption process.

Jim relayed to us that we needed to be fingerprinted again and that this time we should have the prints sent to the INS to Tommy Thorn's attention, who would then expedite them to the FBI (we hoped).

Jack called the Winston-Salem Police Department and told them our story. Although they only took fingerprints on Thursdays from two to four in the afternoon, the officer said he would help us if we came right over. Because Jim had also suggested that we send a letter with our prints, Jack decided to type one out on Krispy Kreme letterhead.

Later, Marie Givner called to wish me a happy birthday. Sensing that I was in no mood for any kind of negative news, she got right to the point: things in Russia were not as bad as we had heard. Despite the threat that had come out of the Kremlin, tensions between America and Russia were unlikely to alter the process of Russian adoption.

Unlikely?

At the end of the day, I tried to console myself further with the thought that all of these difficulties would make our long anticipated first encounter with Alexander even more appreciated and special.

Sad to say, I was glad my birthday was over.

During the first week of December, and despite a bit of a tiff between Clinton and Yeltsin, threats from Russia to prevent American adoptions began to subside. We grew increasingly hopeful that we would have Alexander before Christmas. Jack in particular wanted to bring him with us to Mobile for the holidays to bond with his grandparents, cousins, and other family. All of it hinged on the INS, the FBI, and their sending and processing of our fingerprints.

When Jack spoke with Jim Phillips on the morning of Monday, December 5, he was informed that our fingerprints had not yet been sent back to the INS from the FBI. In an attempt to be encouraging, Jim assured us that once this happened, it would only take three to five days to process the final paperwork. Then, the INS would send a cable to Moscow to let the Russians know that the United States government had approved our adoption.

He said that in cases like ours, the red tape was "cut," and the process was sped up. But given what we had been through with all these agencies, Jack didn't believe him, and neither did I. Jim said he would call the INS back on Wednesday.

The good news was that we had received our visas. Catherine and I spoke of tentative travel plans, particularly about how much time we would need in Moscow to take care of all we needed to do. I spoke to the airline, which had difficulty understanding that four would be traveling to Russia but five would be returning. While the airline clerk loved my story, the airline would not budge on the price of airfare. Oh well, I tried. If all went according to plan, we would be in Moscow by mid-December.

My determination and tenacity rubbed off on Jack. That Wednesday, he called Jim Phillips six times before finally reaching him.

Jim had just gotten through to the INS, but no, our prints had *not* yet been received from the FBI. Jim said he would call back on Thursday.

Jim was a good public servant, and he called the FBI to check on the status on our behalf. He left several voicemails but could not reach anyone with information on the status of the fingerprints until four forty-five that afternoon.

The person at the FBI confirmed that our prints had been processed in late November and sent out shortly thereafter. They would take five to six days to be delivered. In other words, our prints could arrive at the INS later in the week.

We wanted to hear for ourselves the true status of our fingerprints. So Jack called the FBI the next day. By some miracle, the person who answered his call was both helpful and knowledgeable! During their chat, Jack realized that although the fingerprints had been sent to the INS, they were sent bulk mail, which meant that they were packaged with thousands of others.

That evening, Jack and I realized we had to let go and accept that we could not go through with the next week's flight reservations. There was too much up in the air at that point, and our approval could end up taking many more days or weeks. This was especially difficult for Jack. Like us, his family would have to wait to meet Alexander, and, God willing, this would be the last Christmas we would celebrate without him.

8

The Wrecking Ball

Beginning to sink, he [Peter] cried out, "Lord, save me!" Immediately Jesus stretched out his hand and caught him, and said to him, "O you of little faith, why did you doubt?"

—Matthew 14:30–31

On Friday afternoon, I received a phone message from Cheryl, Jack's assistant at Krispy Kreme. She urged me to call her back to hear "some news." When I got her on the phone, she asked, "Do you want to hear it from me or from Jack?"

I said that I had to know *now*. Jim Phillips had called Jack and said that he had once again spoken with Tommy Thorn at the INS. They had received our fingerprints, and our entire package would be processed "in a reasonable period of time."

Breathing a sigh of relief, I thanked Cheryl and hung up.

But after a few fleeting moments of trust, my doubts began to creep in, and I began talking to God, demanding specifics. What was a "reasonable period of time"? A day, a week, a month? There was no clear answer, only silence. While Jack was relieved at the news of the day, I didn't feel that way anymore. I had so many mixed-up feelings. All of a sudden, I was like Peter walking on the water: at first upright, but then sinking, sinking . . .

Would this adoption ever happen? Had I excited everyone I knew for no reason? Would Alexander slip through our fingers? O *me of little faith*! Why was I doubting? Maybe I was just moping again. But I was learning that adoption was a lot like being pregnant: there was excitement and anticipation, but anxiety, difficulty, concern, and exhaustion as well.

On Saturday, the four of us spent the entire day getting Alexander's bedroom ready. We set up bunk beds and outfitted them with new sheets in primary colors with blankets to match. Although it was a small room, it was right in between Lauren and Jennifer's rooms, and he would eventually have his own bathroom.

I say *eventually* because we had begun a major renovation project on our home several months before. At the moment, we had no kitchen; in its place, we used a microwave and a hot plate. On top of it all, the only working bathroom was what would, we hoped, soon be Alexander's. His future bathroom sink was also the only place to wash dishes. Needless to say, we ate out a lot.

The next morning after Mass, we handed Lauren and Jennifer each a wrapped gift. Though they knew exactly what it was, they were excited nonetheless. It was our family tradition. As they unwrapped their gifts, each pulled out a brand-new nutcracker. We turned them upside down and wrote their initials and the year 1994 on the bottom to distinguish them from those from past (and future) years. Later that afternoon, we got dressed up, hopped in the car, and headed to *The Nutcracker* ballet. The girls brought the dolls in their laps.

The Stevens Center was a beautiful theater located in downtown Winston-Salem that the University of North Carolina School of the Arts used for many of their performances. Its beautiful gold curtains and green seats gave it the feel of the best of the past, like a place stuck in time. For our girls, it was magical, and for me, the ballet's Russian origins brought me peace. Between the live orchestra, beautiful scenery, and magnificent costumes, no detail was spared. It was both easy and refreshing to let go of our stress, at least momentarily, and enter into the performance and the Christmas spirit.

The following day, December 12, Jack and I celebrated our thirteenth wedding anniversary. Although it *was* romantic to have been married in December—with candles and Christmas flowers and colors—we now found ourselves struggling year after year to find the opportunity to celebrate our marriage amidst all of the Christmas activities at school and at home.

Tonight, we decided that we would celebrate as a family. This was partly because of the busyness of the season, but also partly because we enjoyed celebrating most things as a family and with as much fun together as possible.

However, this anniversary began a new week, which meant another list of to-dos to bring our son home. Jack spoke with Svetlana that morning.

"Do you have your cable?" she asked, meaning if our approval had been sent to Moscow.

"Well, we are close," Jack guessed—or hoped. We actually had no idea when the INS would get back to us and let us know of our approval.

Svetlana went on to share some details.

First, she said that we should not come to Moscow between Christmas Day and New Year's Day because most Russians typically take off work that week. She indicated it would be better for us to come between New Year's Day and January 7, which was Orthodox Christmas.

Second, her fee for the adoption was $10,000 cash. This fee would cover hotel costs, transportation around Moscow, her agency fee, sightseeing and tourist experiences, the orphanage fee, the translation of the required paperwork, and the gifts for all of the different individuals and groups involved in the adoption process.

At that point, I would have paid just about anything for a guarantee that our son would one day be in our arms, but that didn't erase the strange feeling I got from physically *having* that much cash and then physically *handing* it over to someone else.

We awoke the following day, Wednesday, December 13, with a message from Svetlana on our answering machine to call her at 9:45 a.m. our time.

This time she shared that the chief doctor had met with the Moscow government to get approval for us to adopt Alexander. She said we now had verbal approval and that the written approval would come by the middle of the following week. It was nice to hear that there was someone working on our behalf on the other side of the world!

She needed two things faxed to her as soon as possible. The first was our official application for the adoption. She said that this should communicate that we wished to adopt Alexander, who resided in the Podolsk Children's Home in the Moscow region. We needed to make clear that we were aware of his health conditions and agreed to his diagnosis. The second item she needed was a copy of Catholic Social Services' license for international adoption.

While we had her on the phone, we finally had the opportunity to ask her a few questions that had been swirling in our minds.

Jack asked about the process upon our arrival. Svetlana said that they would pick us up at the airport and take us to our hotel. The following day, we would be driven to Podolsk to meet Sasha. "If you like him," she said, "you will sign some papers and take him with you back to the hotel."

If we like him?

"Of course we will like him!" Jack declared. After all, we had already loved him for months! Jack then asked, "Svetlana, why do you often call Alexander 'Sasha'?"

There was a gentle chuckle on the other end of the phone. "Sasha is the Russian nickname for Alexander, especially when the child is little," Svetlana explained. "The mommas at the orphanage call him Sasha, as he is such a good boy."

Svetlana paused for a moment and then continued, "And there is one more thing you should know. According to the chief doctor, Sasha is living with the teddy bear you sent. He sleeps with him, and he says, 'My mum is Jamie, my dad is Jack, my sisters are Lauren and Jennifer, and I am to live in America, and they are coming soon.' "

Our hearts melted at this amazing revelation. Not only was he living in our hearts, but we were in his.

The call ended with a few cautions. Bring plenty of warm clothes for ourselves and Alexander, as it was snowing and very cold. Bring food too, she said, because Alexander could not eat any bread due to his celiac disease.

After we had hung up the phone and talked through the mountain of information that Svetlana had just shared with us, Jack and I just stared at each other. What kind of food should we bring, and how were we supposed to get it there?

A dilemma for another day.

It was Monday of the next week, December 19. We needed to call Jim that day if we still had not heard from the INS. We had not, of course, so Jack called him as soon as he got to work. Given that our visas were set to expire on January 15, we were anxious to finalize our flights and get to Russia. Jim assured us that he would call the INS, but it would probably be the afternoon before he could reach a person with answers. He joked that they took the phone off the hook until after lunch.

Jim also shared that he would be retiring at the end of December, ending our hopes to bring Alexander by his office once he arrived home. Jack thanked him for all he had done. He had been wonderfully kind and helpful throughout this entire process. We could only imagine all of the people he had helped during his long career.

After a long meeting at work, Jack was talking with his brother, Mac, and coworker, Mike, when Cheryl, Jack's assistant, rushed down the hall with a beaming smile across her face. She announced to all present the news we had been waiting for: Jim Phillips said that our papers had been sent out the previous Friday, and that we should receive news of our approval either that day or the next! Jack called Jim to hear the news for himself, which was such a great relief—or should I say blessing? Thank You, Lord!

Jack asked if the cable stating our approval had been sent to Moscow. Jim didn't know, but he felt sure that it had since that was the procedure. Jack immediately called me, with obvious excitement in his voice as he shared the news. I too was jubilant and about to burst! As you can imagine, we were both on a high for the rest of the day. It was looking like we would get our Christmas present of an INS approval and then be able to make our travel plans to Russia.

Later that afternoon, after meeting with Mac and Mike, Jack took a break to call the INS. Marian Stodger took his call, and Jack shared that we had heard from Jim Phillips the good news that our letter was on the way, and he wanted to check to see if the cable to Moscow had gone out as well. There was a long pause, and Marian asked Jack to hold a minute.

After waiting for what seemed an eternity, she came back to the phone and confirmed that a letter did go out on Friday. However, it was not a letter of approval, but rather one of "intent to deny" from the examiner.

Intent to deny?

Completely blown away, Jack had to take a few seconds to catch his breath. He then asked, "What does this mean?"

Marian told Jack that the examiner had reviewed our case, and based on something in the packet, he refused to approve our adoption at this time.

Despite the wrecking ball that had just swept through our plans, Jack tried to remain calm and clear minded.

"Marian, how can this be true? What's the problem?"

"I'm sorry, Mr. McAleer, but I'm not allowed to discuss any case over the phone. You should receive your certified letter in the mail today that will explain the reasons for the denial."

Jack tried to suppress his anger, fear, and disbelief. "Is this something that can be corrected?" he asked.

"I'm sorry, Mr. McAleer. I can't say. Upon receipt of your letter, you have fifteen days to respond."

Jack's mind raced as he hung up the phone. He immediately called Jim Phillips, who could not believe what he was hearing. The INS gave no hint that the letter we were receiving was anything other than a letter of acceptance. Unfortunately, there was nothing that he could do because his role was only to help push the case through.

Jack thanked Jim again and hung up the phone.

What do we do now? swirled round and round in Jack's mind. *How do I break this news to Jamie?*

9

Animal Cookies

In you, Lord, I take refuge;
let me never be put to shame.

—Psalm 71:1

Jack knew it was time to get home and somehow find the calm and the courage to let me know this devastating news. At the time, though, I was not at home, but at school for Jennifer's Christmas party. In the meantime, Jack was able to catch up with Catherine and tell her the story of what he had heard.

Catherine could not believe it. She could not imagine *why* we would have been denied. "Could it have been something in the FBI investigation?" she asked.

"No way," Jack said. But then—perhaps through a nudge of the Holy Spirit—he remembered an incident when I was a junior at Auburn University. He gave Catherine a brief rundown of what had happened and asked if this could be the problem.

"It's possible," she stated, sounding unsure. "I've seen it once before. I'll call Marie and as soon as she can, have her call you."

A short time later, I arrived home early with Lauren, who wasn't feeling well. Jack chose not to say anything at first, but I sensed that something was wrong. As Lauren ate her lunch, Jack asked me to come upstairs with him. With each step, my anxiety increased. When we reached the top of the stairs, Jack told me about his conversation with the INS and what he suspected about the FBI report and the Auburn incident. No cable was being sent to Moscow. The letter and its official denial, he said, would arrive today.

My mind reeled, and my heart pounded. The room spun, and the weight of a sudden hopelessness pressed in on me. Could something as innocent and foolish as a college shenanigan cause me to lose my child? This was a nightmare, a terror of the worst kind, an instant depression, and, again, God was seemingly absent or far-off. How on earth was I to get through these next few hours waiting for the certified letter to arrive with our verdict—*the denial of the adoption of our son?*

In 1980, I was a junior at Auburn University and still a "little sister" to Jack's fraternity, Sigma Phi Epsilon. As it happened, I had a bit of a say as to which of the brothers became my official "big brother," and I think it goes without saying which of them I wanted. However, Jack's good friends in the fraternity also became my big brothers in a greater and more meaningful way. Of course, there were a few loudmouths around that I was a bit scared of and didn't want to associate with, but Jack's closest friends were always nice to me, even protective. I was always treated with nothing but respect, which was especially true of Jack.

Jack's friends were fun and kind, and since I never had a brother of my own, these guys filled the role perfectly. There was one semester in particular in which Jack had gone to live at home and work at his father's Krispy Kreme store to earn money for school, though he would often come up and see us all on the weekends.

Although we weren't officially dating at this time, we were certainly an "item," and his brothers watched after me. At least they tried.

One Friday afternoon, two of these brothers and I went on what was supposed to be a fun excursion to the Super Foods grocery store in Auburn to buy something (I can't even remember what). But I do remember the three of us walking through the store, looking at all the grocery items, and laughing together. At one point, one of us picked up a box of animal cookies, opened it, and began eating from it. Then, without giving it much thought, we put the box down and kept shopping.

Eventually clarity set in, and I thought, *I better go back and get that box and pay for it*, but after retracing our steps through the store, I could not find it. Thinking it would be redemptive, I picked up another box and went to the checkout. We paid for the animal cookies along with the rest of our groceries and left the store, only to discover a police officer waiting for us just outside the entrance. Just like that, we found ourselves in the back of a police car and on the way to the station.

I do not have much memory of what happened from that moment on and at the police station, most likely because I had blocked it out. I do know, though, that we were photographed and jailed—and fingerprinted.

Despite my humiliation, I had to call my sorority advisor. She and her husband came right away and picked me up and took me back to my dorm. I cried there in the darkness of my room, thinking that at this point Jack would *never* love me and that my parents would *never* forgive me. Fortunately, both fears were ungrounded. Jack was both comforting and understanding, and he shared in my suffering as best he could while being upset about the whole incident right along with me. My parents were surprisingly wonderful and supportive. My mom consulted her brother, my Uncle George, who was an attorney. Shortly thereafter, they hired a local lawyer to help us figure this scenario out.

Apparently, Super Foods was tired of college students playing around in their store. I learned of another girl who had been arrested for eating grapes from a bunch to see if they were sweet prior to purchasing them. From what we could ascertain, Super Foods wanted to make an example of a few to discourage the rest. Apparently, I was one of those examples.

Despite the support of family and friends, this whole experience was mortifying. I was not the kind of girl to break the rules, at least not on purpose. To be treated like a criminal for a mistake (one that I had even tried to rectify!) was over the top.

Fortunately, all charges on us were dismissed.

Long story short, because I was under twenty-one, I was treated as such under the "juvenile offender law." Supposedly my files had been sealed, and in the eyes of the courts, this event had never happened. I was advised by my lawyer to *never* think of or mention this truly embarrassing incident again. And I never did, even when we were going through the paperwork for our adoption. I had completely wiped it from my memory.

Now, fifteen years later, this incident had resurfaced. It had come back to haunt me, unleashing a pain far greater than mere humiliation. At first, disbelief gave way to depression. Now, after a minute of the worst sorrow, the depression gave way to anger. I lost it. I was so angry and disgusted. I started yelling and screaming. Lauren and Jack probably thought I had lost my mind. Perhaps I did for a minute or two—or maybe five.

Any thoughts of God or faith or trust were pushed away, but Jack was able to calm me down. Lauren held my hand as I cried.

Sam nestled in my lap. Jack stayed until Lauren and I had to leave at three o'clock to pick up Jennifer from school. Somehow, I managed to do this, and even brought Jennifer to meet with her Brownie troop, albeit in a daze. When we arrived home, I noticed a yellow card with the rest of the mail stating that he, the mailman, still had our letter. Because it was certified, he had to give it to us in person.

I knew I had to have that letter. Now.

I put the girls back into the car and drove around the neighborhood, looking for the mailman. I was very close with my daughters, and they knew me well enough to know that I was on a mission. Imagine Cruella de Vil in Disney's *101 Dalmatians* as she crazily, yet purposefully, careened after the truck carrying the dalmatians. Now remember the look on her face, how it was determined but awful and very scary? I'm certain that's how I looked, because that is exactly how I felt.

First, we drove to the post office, but our mailman hadn't returned yet. We turned around and drove around our area some more. I was on a hunt, but after what seemed like hundreds of turns and streets and false alarms, there wasn't a mail truck in sight.

When we got back to the post office, they were closing the gates; all of the trucks had come through and were parked for the evening. I drove up to the lady who was closing them, and as briefly—yet a bit emotionally—as I could, I poured out my story. She listened patiently, and when I had finished, she said she would help me since it was the "holiday season." Amazingly, she retrieved the certified letter and handed it to me.

But I couldn't bring myself to open it just then.

10

True Faith

Yes, when you seek me with all your heart, I will let you find me . . . and I will change your lot.

—Jeremiah 29:13–14

When Jack got home, I told him that the letter was on the hall table. I could not bring myself to open it alone. When our hopes for another child were dashed by infertility, it was together. When we fell in love with Alexander, it was together. If our dreams of adopting him were going to be officially ruined, it would be together. He picked it up, and the two of us walked to the sunroom. Jack opened the envelope, and, as we both suspected, the reason for the "intent to deny" was the FBI report. I was, at least in the eyes of the INS examiner, a criminal.

On the way to pick up pizza for dinner, Jack called Barrie Renshaw at Petree Stockton law firm, the group of lawyers for Krispy Kreme. He told her the whole story and asked if she would help us get the files from the court in Auburn. Barrie quickly assured Jack that she would do all she could to help us sort through this, but she also shared that, in her experience, once the U.S. government issued its "decree" of approval or denial, it rarely changed its mind.

Jack decided not to share this bit of information with me quite yet. However, Krispy Kreme, upon learning the situation, made it clear that if necessary, Jack could use the company plane to get himself or any documents from here to there.

Barrie asked Jack to drop off a copy of the letter in the morning to her office, and she would get right on it. Instead of consulting with a local law firm in Auburn, she said she would first try direct communication with the court itself.

It was a rough night with a lot of tossing and turning.

Oh, Alexander! Have I lost you, my son? I heard his voice again; he was calling to me, waiting for me, and encouraging me not to give up.

When morning finally arrived, I got ready and the four of us hopped in the car. The girls couldn't believe that I had pulled myself together and that I was going with their dad to the law firm. When we arrived at school, Lauren leaned over to her dad and whispered, "I'll be praying for you!"

Jack, the softie that he was, teared up.

When we arrived, we handed Barrie all our papers, and she began to fax letters everywhere. Meanwhile, Marie was working on a response letter to the INS and would send it out as soon as she heard from Barrie, who was waiting for the courtroom in Auburn to open for the day.

Barrie believed that the INS was more concerned that we had not disclosed the incident to Catholic Social Services and the home study rather than with the incident itself. After Barrie asked some specific questions about what had happened at Auburn, Jack called Cheryl to see if the Krispy Kreme plane was available over the next few days—just in case we needed to get somewhere fast.

After school, I had to take the girls with me back to Petree Stockton to sign a form to release my records. There, Barrie asked me many more questions. What did I remember about the case? How did I plead? Of course, as a matter of thorough protocol, she had to ask me all these questions. She needed the facts because she was concerned for us. However, the same criminal feelings I had all of those years ago in the dark of my dorm room, escalated by conversations with my parents and my Uncle George, came rushing back.

How could I have done something so stupid? But then again, it was so simple, so harmless; it was as innocent as a small prank or an accident.

She said that INS didn't care what I did, only that I had tried to conceal it. For that alone, they could deny us. I was so upset, and I knew my face reflected it. I told Barrie that I thought I was going to get an ulcer.

The girls and I went home. I was struggling to maintain my composure. We were supposed to go to a friend's house and bake Christmas cookies, but I knew I couldn't handle that. I was trying to keep a smile and a Christmas spirit for Lauren and Jennifer, but it was just too hard. So finally I called Jack and started to cry. He said he would come home right away.

Then I called Marie, and, as she had many times before, she did her best to comfort me. By the time Jack arrived home, I was feeling a bit better, or at least I was composed. He played with the girls, and I joined them. Fifteen minutes later, the phone rang.

Barrie was on the other line, and, though Jack was the first to answer, she wanted to speak with me. She said that all of the information had come in from Auburn, and I was right! I *had* been treated under the juvenile offender law, and my records were (supposedly) sealed. In fact, the judge who had seen my case was still there. I had acted correctly. I should never have disclosed anything.

"Then how," I pressed, "did the FBI get access to my fingerprints from Auburn that were supposedly sealed?"

She wasn't sure. There must have been a mistake somewhere. Barrie assured me not to worry, that she and many others were taking care of everything. Marie's response letter and Barrie's legal letter and other documents would be processed by the state in Raleigh and ultimately pushed back into the hands of the INS in Charlotte for their approval.

Jack and I cried tears of relief—and hope. I decided to take the girls to my friend's house to decorate cookies after all. Afterward, we went to dinner as a family to "celebrate" this hopeful bit of news. When Barrie called later that night, she stressed it would be up to us to physically pick up the necessary documents from Raleigh and deliver them to the INS building in Charlotte so they could be processed as soon as possible.

It looked like we would need the Krispy Kreme plane after all.

On December 22, Jack awoke around five in the morning, quietly got out of bed, and got dressed. He was raised in the doughnut business to be an early riser; I was not. However, this morning I was up too. It was quiet, and I was surprisingly calm, as if in the eye of the storm. I had the coffee ready and asked Jack if he wanted some, but he said no; he would have some on the plane. I kissed him on the cheek on his way out the door.

A little while later, I spoke with Catherine, who was all fired up. I filled her in as matter-of-factly as I was able, and she asked a few more questions, which I answered to her satisfaction. When all this was finished, she said she wanted to issue a formal complaint to the Atlanta branch of the INS about the Charlotte branch. This soothed my hurting heart and somewhat satisfied my personal and motherly indignation.

On his way to the airport, Jack began to wonder if everything was going to work as planned. He had not heard from Barrie regarding any changes, so he assumed that the original plan was still in place: fly to Raleigh, grab the papers, fly to Charlotte, deliver them to the INS.

Jack arrived at the airport at 5:45 a.m. and was greeted by Kelly and Marilyn, Krispy Kreme's pilots, who were ready to help him any way they could. Once aboard, Jack sipped coffee and calmly reflected on what the day might bring.

They arrived in Raleigh on schedule. However, as the plane pulled up to the terminal, Kelly came over the speaker with a message that had just come through: the papers needed were no longer in Raleigh but had been delivered the night before to Winston-Salem.

Jack got off the plane and called Mac, who said that Barrie had tried to get him all evening but never got an answer. Jack remembered that we had been out much of the evening, and, because we were so set on the plan, we hadn't checked the phone for any messages. Mac had also tried to reach him and to catch him at the airport before he left, but, because they had left so early, he missed them.

Jack quickly called Barrie, and she apologized and said she would meet him at the Winston-Salem airport. Jack reboarded, and the plane turned around, landing in Winston-Salem around 6:50 a.m. Barrie was there, as promised.

She handed him the envelope, saying, "All you need to tell the INS is that when the Auburn incident went to court, Jamie was told to treat it as though it never happened, and that she was protected by the juvenile offender law." She concluded by saying that the same judge who was there those years ago wrote a letter to clear my record.

On the flight to Charlotte, envelope on his lap, Jack reflected on all we had been through together to get to this point. We had not been married long but had already been through our share of hardships and blessings. When the plane landed, Jack hopped in the rental car and began the relatively short drive to the INS offices.

With a renewed determination to make this change happen, Jack decided to make a quick stop and get a couple dozen Krispy Kreme doughnuts to bring to the INS. He had witnessed the power of the doughnut before at store openings in dozens of cities. It had landed him on television and backed up traffic on the interstate. It had gripped popular culture and incited something just shy of mass hysteria in many places. Today he was hoping that maybe these doughnuts could help soften the hearts of a few government officials.

He was resolved that he would not leave until he had spoken with someone, a real person who had some kind of authority or power over our situation—and doughnuts always seemed to help make that happen.

Jack pulled into the INS parking lot around 7:45 a.m. With warm doughnuts in hand, he entered the two-story office building and found that there were already people in line ahead of him. He took a number, seventeen, and sat down. The room was quiet and dotted with anonymous strangers, most of whom cast a sort of curious (though probably desirous) glance in Jack's direction. If they didn't recognize the green-speckled box, then it was the sweet smell of warm sugar that grabbed their attention.

After only a little waiting, his number was called.

Jack asked to speak with Tommy Thorn, since he was the one who signed the certified letter with the "intent to deny" our adoption. The officer behind the desk asked Jack if he had ever spoken with Mr. Thorn.

"Yes," Jack replied, a little loose on the truth. He then handed the officer the letter we had received from Mr. Thorn, a picture of Alexander, the reply from the Department of Human Resources in Raleigh, the papers from Catholic Social Services, the letter from the judge in Auburn to clear my name, the legal papers from Barrie, and, lastly, the two dozen doughnuts. The officer took all of these things to the back room, came back a few minutes later, and asked Jack to be seated.

Twenty minutes later, someone from the back of the room shouted out, "Jack McAleer!" Jack hopped up and followed the man who had called his name. Once through the door, Jack informed the man that he was there to speak with Mr. Thorn.

"That's me," the man said. "Come this way."

Jack was escorted to a corner office and saw the papers lying across Thorn's desk. As they took their seats, Thorn asked, "What is this about?"

So Jack began to tell him our story—about our desire to adopt Alexander, about our visas that were soon to expire, and, most importantly, about the mix-up regarding the Auburn incident.

"Is everything you're telling me in written form?" Thorn asked. "Yes, it's all there," Jack replied as he pointed to the top of the desk.

Thorn fingered the various papers and cast a glance at Jack. "Are you under the impression that I am going to approve this paperwork here and now, today?"

"Sir," Jack replied. "We have been very patient through this entire process, and we would have already been approved if it were not for the FBI mistake."

"Just so you know, I can't approve this," Thorn replied. "But I will pass it on to the examiner for approval or denial."

Jack said, "I assumed it was up to you, sir, since it was your signature on the intent to deny that we received in the mail."

Mr. Thorn was very prickly; his name fit him well. After a quiet moment, he mumbled that he would see what he could do. Jack wished him a Merry Christmas and thanked him in advance for assisting us in the effort to adopt Alexander. Jack was shown the way out.

As my husband left Tommy Thorn's office and the INS building, he reflected again on what a journey this had been. He was blown away at how some aspects of our government could be so unfeeling, almost as if there were no heart or soul in some of the people who worked in it.

But there was still hope. We had done all that was humanly possible to do, and now it was out of our hands. The future and fate of our son, yet again, rested in the hands of the U.S. government, and, of course, in God's as well.

Though we couldn't bring Alexander to Mobile for Christmas, we could leave the process itself behind for the first time in months. What a blessing it was to be surrounded by Jack's family, many of whom had bought gifts for Alexander. All of them, Jack's parents and siblings and nieces and nephews, carried a sense of love and peace that was contagious. Jack shared with a few of them our latest "boulders," and they spread the story so that everyone would know. I didn't want too many questions, or to explain my side of things over and over if I didn't have to.

However, when I did feel like it was helpful to talk, I would bring it up. At one point during our visit, Jack and I vented our most recent struggles with Buster, our brother-in-law, who was an attorney.

"Well, Jamie," he said, "you're just a criminal!"

The laughter was just what we needed. I opened up a bit more and asked him how on earth the FBI had gotten a hold of my fingerprints when they were supposed to have been sealed up, apparently forever. He said it was probably a mistake, that someone—a clerk perhaps—had put them in the wrong stack, and they went to the FBI. Though it helped to hear this, I was still angry about how one small mistake by an anonymous clerk could fail and hurt me and my family so much, keeping a young boy from the mother and father he deserved.

Early on Christmas Eve morning, I suffered a relapse of sorts, back into the anxiety and struggle of this tumultuous process that had hurt me in ways I never would have anticipated. I had prayed for signs, and I was struck with pain instead. I asked God for help, but was given none that I could see. My heart had made room for my son, and he had found a home there, until now.

I hid myself in the bathroom and for the first time since the "intent to deny" had occurred, prayed to God with honesty—from the heart. *How can I possibly trust You, Lord?* I was Hannah again, drunkenly exhorting God on behalf of a child. I was Sarah, doubting that God could or would be a Father who lived up to His promises. I was Rebekah, the object of everyone's prayers. I was Rachel, crying out for a child through tears and pain. *Where are You?*

There was a soft knock on the bathroom door. I opened it slowly and saw the gentle face of Jack's mom on the other side. She saw me and my look of pain and could read my heart like only a mother could. I don't remember exactly what she said as she handed me two prayer cards, but it was something simple like, "I wanted you to have these."

What I do remember was the content of the cards. The first, about healing, was well-timed and much needed. The second card, titled "To Our Lady," had a beautiful picture of Our Blessed Mother on the front and a prayer on the back.

As I read and studied this second prayer card, I realized that my mother-in-law, whom I loved very much, had just brought me hope, the antidote to anxiety. God had heard my pleas and had sent me—through her—not another sign or a promise, but the means to surrender everything to the Lord through His Mother. There was no one left to turn to but God and Our Blessed Mother, not for answers but for *peace*.

Right then I made a promise to the Mother of Jesus and of us all: if she helped me get my son, I would give her all of the credit. I would get to know *her* better, and through her, *her Son*.

Now the second part of the prayer from Jeremiah that I had prayed so many months ago needed to be lived out:

> Yes, when you seek me with all your heart, I will let you find me ... and I will change your lot; I will gather you together from all the nations and all the places to which I have banished you ... and bring you back to the place from which I have exiled you. (Jer. 29:13–14)

Up to this point in my life, I had only a shallow relationship with Our Blessed Mother. As a Protestant, I knew little of her, and as a relatively new Catholic, I had never intentionally developed a relationship with her. She was an unapproachable personage, like a figurehead or an image of Catholicism. But now I desperately needed and wanted her help. I ached for her compassion and intervention in my dire situation. She too, after all, is a *mother*.

I also promised her that I would place this prayer card to her and her Son on Alexander's adoption announcement—if that would ever come to pass. This offer seemed so simple, feeble even, but at this moment of my journey it was the best that I could come up with. And I needed to pray this prayer *with all my heart.*

There—crumpled on the bathroom floor—I prayed the prayer printed on the back of the holy card:

> Lovely Lady dressed in blue, teach me how to pray;
> God was just your little boy, tell me what to say.
> Did you lift him up sometimes, gently on your knee?
> Did you sing to him the way Mother does to me?
> Did you hold his hand at night?
> Did you ever try telling stories of the World? O, and did he cry?
> Do you really think he cares if I tell him things—little things that happen?
> And, do the angel's wings make a noise? Can he hear me if I speak low?
> Does he understand me now? Tell me, for you know.
> Lovely Lady dressed in blue, teach me how to pray.
> God was just your little boy, and you know the way.
> (Our Lady of the Assumption Prayer)

I had been raised Christian. If anyone had ever asked, I would have said that I had a relationship with God. The Bible was at my bedside, and I had attended church every Sunday of my life with rare exception. I was morally upright and, in the eyes of all who knew me, a good woman and a good mother. But there on a bathroom floor, I was finally given the full depth of a gift that had been bestowed upon me in baptism: *faith.*

I left the entire situation in Mary's hands.

11

The Miracle

The loveliest masterpiece of the heart of God is the heart of a mother.

—St. Thérèse of Lisieux

On the Tuesday after Christmas, we arrived back in Winston-Salem. Though happy to be home, I was quickly reminded of all the phone calls and home visits and the multitude of worrying and waiting that we had left behind. When we left, I thought I'd have to pick it right back up and be wrought with anxiety yet again, but things were different. God was relying on us, but I was for the first time relying on Him.

We were to call the INS the next morning. One more night of tossing, turning, and hoping, but also one last chance for Our Blessed Mother to carry my plea to her Son.

The moment the office opened on Wednesday, Jack called to see if there had possibly been a decision in our case. Had it been approved? He waited while it rang, was transferred, then waited some more. All that we had been through—unending phone calls, nervousness, fear, excitement, drama, and denials—were rolled up into these tense moments for the both of us.

Jack had a tight grip on the phone, his face more tense than usual, not daring to move lest he miss something or someone. I darted about our house doing little things that really didn't need doing, but I had to do *something,* punctuating my activity with deep and heartfelt prayer: *Please, Lovely Lady Dressed in Blue, help us, please.*

I have been told that every secret wish is a prayer, and I was "wishing" very hard. We both waited for what seemed like hours for the right person to pick up so we could ask our momentous question. At long last, Jack was able to put forth his query: *What was the status of the McAleer adoption?* The person he spoke to on the phone paused for a moment and shuffled through some paperwork on his desk. Finally, he shared the ultimate verdict that we had so longingly waited *and prayed* for:

Approved!

When the INS employee said that our approval letter would be sent in the mail, Jack instinctively cried out, "No! Wait! We will come and pick it up! No, not tomorrow, we'll come right now!"

The U.S. government had changed its mind and cleared us to go to Russia and bring home our son. This was a miracle! *Thank you, Lovely Lady Dressed in Blue!*

As fast as humanly possible, Jack, Lauren, Jennifer, and I hopped in our car and drove to Charlotte, rejoicing in disbelief all the way. I couldn't believe it. I simply couldn't believe it. I kept asking Jack, "What if they mixed us up with someone else?"

O Lord, please forgive my lack of faith!

We arrived in Charlotte in record time. I believe angels must have helped carry us. This was my first time at the INS office, which was just as Jack had described it: small and dreary. Still, even the smallest and dreariest of offices would have looked beautiful that day. We were handed our approval letter. We had our son. Case closed.

Now, to celebrate at the Original Pancake House for a late breakfast!

Despite never leaving the state of North Carolina, at least on official adoption business, it had been a journey. However, now the journey was to become an adventure. We were off to Moscow to find and bring our son home.

We had one week.

Jack made his preparations to be gone from work while I scrambled around at home—going from room to room and bag to bag checking and double checking. On Wednesday, January 4, 1995, the four of us piled into the car to travel, yet again, to Charlotte for our flight, this time a bit cramped by all of the bags.

We had twelve bags in total. Thanks to a suggestion from Marie, one of them contained nothing but food—cookies, crackers, and Capri-Suns for the girls, and gluten-free snacks (as best I could find back then) for Alexander. Another contained the gifts and trinkets—many of them Krispy Kreme themed—we had been encouraged to bring with us for the children in the orphanage and anyone else we might interact with. We weren't sure who these people would be, but we were prepared.

We arrived at the Charlotte airport in plenty of time. After checking in, we went to the gate and met the Barker family, who had graciously come to give us a hug of support and courage. They also brought along their new daughter, Michelle, whom Pat had spoken of on the phone. She was a beautiful and healthy little girl with a pretty round face, rosy cheeks, big happy eyes, and wispy brown hair. This was a boost of encouragement, hope, and confidence for the four of us.

They also shared some suggestions. They warned us not to travel alone on the subway (known as the Metro), as this could be dangerous. We should allow Svetlana's daughter, Jenny, to help us get the rubles we needed—another bit of sound advice. They confided that they only gave Svetlana the $10,000 after they met Michelle and had agreed to take her home. If we needed a bathroom, the hotels would be the place to go. Finally, they encouraged us to call them at any hour if we had questions or needed anything, and they wanted to meet us at the airport upon our return.

This was all very comforting, but that golden event seemed years away. If the American government had been difficult to deal with, what could it possibly be like working with the Russians?

We said goodbye and eventually boarded the plane and got settled in for the long flight. The girls smiled with excitement and were fascinated by the headphones that could be plugged into the seats in front of them.

Suddenly, Jennifer turned a bit downcast, leaned over to me, and said, "I think I'm going to miss my turn to be line leader and table washer."

Oh, to have such simple and humble worries! But at that moment, fear and concern as a parent washed over me. What was I doing to my daughters, who were just seven and nine years old? Why was I separating them from the comfort of their home and routine and taking them on a risky and speculative journey into unknown territory?

However, Jack and I wanted them to share in this momentous experience. We wanted them to *see, know, understand—and always remember.* We weren't a family without them.

And little did we know how much we would need them—and soon.

After traveling nearly a dozen hours from Charlotte to Munich and from Munich to Moscow, we were mentally preparing to land in Russia and settling into the fact that we were nearly there. The girls had been troopers, but we were all exhausted.

Just before landing, we were given declaration forms by the crew members and were told to declare what we were carrying into the country. Jack and I looked at each other in a panic: What do we say about the $10,000 cash we were bringing in for the adoption? For all the advice we had received—from bathrooms to blue jeans—no one had said anything about this. Soon we would be departing the plane. *Should we lie?* No, that would be terrible for us if we were searched. *Should we tell the truth?* It was easy to imagine that in these times the Russians might find it suspicious that Americans were carrying that much cash into their country. What should we do?

What on earth do we write on this ominous piece of paper sitting in front of us?

As we sweated in our seats, we realized that the forms were just for Jack and myself, not for our daughters. So, I took the $10,000 out of my bag and put it into Jennifer's backpack. She would carry the money into Russia for us. Jack and I could now declare what we were bringing into the country—our clothes, some Krispy Kreme trinkets, and a suitcase of food.

At that moment, I felt like Rahab, ancestor of Jesus, who not only acted on faith but did so with tremendous risk to her own life. As she hid the spies of Joshua, I hid the money. She feared the king, and I feared this recently non-Communist government. She knew the might of God, and I knew that He had not brought us this far for nothing. With faith, she saved her family, and with faith, I was hoping to unite mine.

As we got off the plane, I immediately noticed that the Moscow airport looked fifty years behind those in America. It was old, drab, and dingy. Even the lights were dim, giving us the feeling of walking in a constant shadow.

We huddled closely as we made our way through the corridor and down the escalator.

Beyond the security gate, we were relieved to lay eyes on who we thought (and hoped) were our local support—our tour guides waving to us from the other side.

Svetlana and those who were with her were like icons of Russia itself, beautifully dressed in their furs and bundled from head to toe. As we got closer, it was probably apparent that we were exhausted and, to be honest, a bit scared of customs and the Russia that waited for us beyond this worn-out, old building.

When we finally reached them, Svetlana quickly eased our fears, helped us relax, and even caused us to crack a smile. She was a jolly, middle-aged woman with a round face and rosy cheeks. Her dark hair was piled on top of her head, and she was attired in fur from her hat down to her boots. To Lauren and Jennifer, she looked like Mrs. Claus. To our great comfort, she spoke English very well with a beautiful Russian accent.

She introduced us to Jenny, her daughter, who was in her early twenties. Blessedly, she spoke English as well as her mother. She was very pretty, with a gentle look and touch. Lauren and Jennifer liked her right away, especially the attention she gave them.

Svetlana helped us to get through customs without any problems, retrieve our luggage, and find our driver. We quickly understood that she was savvy, in business as well as life. Not only was she the owner of the Victoria Tourist House, but she knew exactly what to do and where to go. On top of it all, people listened to her as if she were in command.

Our first and only stop was our hotel, and Svetlana talked with us all the way there. "Tomorrow you will see Sasha, okay?" she assured us, using the affectionate nickname we had all come to love, all in her loud, jolly way.

Jack and I looked at each other: Okay! That's why we were here!

I couldn't wait to get to our hotel but was apprehensive about what we would find once we arrived.

As we approached the Hotel Ukraine, we were intimidated by the large and domineering statue out front. Whoever he was, he stood tall with his hands behind his back and cape blowing in the cold wind. This dark sculpture seemed to lean over us, over Russia itself, as if it were a warning to all visitors. Was it Lenin, Stalin, or some other imposing figure poised to keep an eye on us over his thick mustache?

Not far from where we stood, smoke billowed from the factories along the river. After passing beneath a large hammer and sickle, which adorned the rooftop, we entered the hotel. Though it was warmer inside than out, the large, cold marble lobby made me shudder. In the middle of this vestibule stood a tall, skinny, and very dead Christmas tree flanked by a few smaller ones of the same type. As we passed by, we noticed the sparse ornaments and the thousands of needles that littered the floor. I thought of our tree back home and felt the sting of homesickness.

According to one of our guides, our hotel was referred to as one of the "Seven Ugly Sisters," which had been built by Stalin following World War II. Apparently, he loved Gothic architecture, particularly the spires that characterized that style. Exhibiting both, the Hotel Ukraine was a perfect example of Stalinist architecture. Beautiful yes, but not the most welcoming.

Upon check-in, we were asked to hand over our passports. This made Jack and I very nervous. What if they lost or damaged them? However, we followed the advice we were given by those who had done this before us, and we did as we were told.

Svetlana and Jenny escorted us to our rooms, which were next door to each other but not connected, and helped us to give out appropriate tips to the bellhops. Each room had a refrigerator and a bathroom, but the amenities were lacking. The bed linens were a story in themselves, being made of a rough linen fabric—no soft cotton or sateen here. However, given our exhaustion, anything would have felt good that night.

Svetlana and Jenny hugged us and said that they would see us at nine the next morning to go see Alexander. Before they left, Svetlana warned us to lock our doors and not to open them at all during the night. Not exactly the most comforting goodbye.

We were all alone in a Russian hotel.

Jennifer was beginning to fall apart, and I knew she was hungry. While we had the suitcase full of snacks, we all needed something more substantial. The four of us went searching and finally discovered a small cafe-style restaurant on the third floor. After much maneuvering with the Russian language, we managed to order and pay for some borscht soup, a little bit of meat, some bread, and a couple of soft drinks. After devouring this simple and nourishing supper, the girls felt much better.

However, Jack was distracted throughout dinner, thinking through Svetlana's warning. How could we be split between the two rooms, and was it even a good idea in the first place? As we made our way back upstairs for the night, Jack made an executive decision.

We pulled the two paper-thin mattresses and bedding from one of the rooms into the other, and we all slept together—kind of like a big sleepover party. As we were getting settled into these new sleeping arrangements, the phone in the room rang.

Because we were already anxious, and given that this was our final night as a family of four, it startled us all. Jack picked it up, and I heard him say, "No, thank you. We're fine."

He hung up the phone, looked at me, and said, "Housekeeping wanted to know if we needed anything."

Well, that was a nice gesture, I thought. It was much, much later that Jack shared with me the truth of these phone calls, which would come every night of our stay.

A woman with a deep, husky voice and Russian accent would ask, "Handsome American man want sex with Russian woman?"

And every night, Jack would answer, "No, thank you. We're fine."

Though sleep came easily given how tired we were, I could not help but think of my son, sleeping in the orphanage, waiting for me. Had he been ordered to bed that night after a meal that didn't suit him? Had he been sung a lullaby or given a good night kiss?

We're coming, son. We're coming.

12

Meeting Our Son

I prayed for this child, and the LORD granted my request.

—1 Samuel 1:27

We were so excited and nervous that we were all up at six that Friday morning. This was a mistake, for by the time Svetlana and Jenny arrived, we were all tired and sick. Jennifer especially so, who complained of feeling nauseous until she finally threw up as the excitement, lack of sleep, and strange food caught up with her.

Though I too was feeling ill, it wasn't physical. I was terrified about what would be happening that day, and just like the labor of giving birth, wondered how I would make it to the other side with my child in my arms.

But Jennifer and Lauren—troopers that they were—pulled themselves together, and we all boarded an old, white minivan and began our hour-long journey to Podolsk, an industrial city south of Moscow. The roads out of the capital were wide but without lanes or perhaps even laws. Cars swerved within inches of each other as they dodged pothole after crumbling pothole, which dotted the highways.

Although it was not snowing that morning, there was a lot of snow on the ground and it was very cold outside. The van was warm, though, and both Lauren and Jennifer slept for most of the trip. I, on the other hand, was far from comfortable and was overflowing with nerves. Despite having been on the ground in Russia for less than twenty-four hours, my anxiety was taking control. I felt like I was having a panic attack. I was ready to tell Svetlana, "Just take the $10,000 and give me my son and let me go home."

Just like during the labor of our daughters, I was squeezing Jack's hand so hard that I'm sure it was sore later that evening.

After what seemed like ages, we turned down a smaller side road, then down what looked to be an alley. These streets were ruled by wild dogs who watched us suspiciously as the van rumbled past. If it weren't for the playground, it would have been difficult to tell that we had arrived at an orphanage. Before us was a large, old, burnt yellow building, looking more like an old, dilapidated farmhouse than a home for children. White iron bars fanned out from the corners of many of the windows.

We were there. The time had come.

Without hesitation, everyone began climbing out of the van. Doubts hemmed me in on every side as if to throw me back into the vehicle. *What were we doing? Who in their right mind does this? Maybe all of those who had criticized us were right!* But despite my worries, all I could do was move forward in faith, which meant out of the car and onto the gravel driveway of the Podolsk orphanage.

The snow from the previous day had iced a bit and crunched beneath our feet as we drew closer to the threshold of the orphanage. Our crew was greeted at the door by an older woman wearing a white coat and a tall, white hat, who I was informed was the principal. Although at the moment I didn't have much time to take it all in, I could easily tell that the inside of the place was no better cared for than the outside. We were ushered up a flight of stairs and eventually taken into an office-like waiting room where we took off our coats, hats, scarves, and gloves.

Inside there were many heavy Russian ladies, known as the "mommas." Most of them wore rumpled, white housecoats and what looked like bedroom slippers. They sported no makeup and had messy, pulled-back hair. They watched us as if we were from another world—and I guess we were. Relaxed, these ladies were not. What a commotion! All around us women were moving, directing, and keeping busy as some combination of English and Russian phrases bounced off the walls.

We were ushered out of this little place and up more stairs and into what seemed to be yet another waiting room. This house was bigger than we thought, but felt empty. When we asked, "Where are all the children?" we learned that they had gone out for a New Year's party and would be back soon. Before we could even sit a minute and take a deep breath, one of the ladies came in and announced in Russian, "Come and see: Alexander is a doctor!"

As we were led on this next excursion through the orphanage, my senses were heightened for any sight of my son, and I was more attentive. Svetlana was in front of me as we traveled up and down and around corners, and, as we went, we passed many rooms filled with cribs and beds. I was glad there were no children in them at the moment; it would have been too overwhelming and distracting.

Svetlana rounded a corner, then turned to me with a smile.

I saw a small, pale face peeking around an open door down the hall. He was wearing a white doctor coat over a red-striped shirt and a hat with a red cross in its center. Underneath he had on pink pants that seemed to spring from the smallest of little red shoes that gripped his feet.

My first feelings were all jumbled, held in by a blur of tears. Here he was, the realization of the hope that I was given on a bathroom floor.

All around me the women swirled, but I was frozen. Though the mommas spoke to Alexander in Russian, I could make out words common to both languages: *momma, poppa, sistra*. Jack did not hesitate. He went right up to the little doctor, scooped him up in his large hands, and carried him into the center of what must have been the playroom. Lauren, Jennifer, and I gathered around Alexander as he sat on his dad's knee.

Lauren and Jennifer were shy at first, maybe more like awe-struck. This boy we had been speaking and dreaming of for months was suddenly more than just an idea or an image on a Polaroid. He was here before them, living and breathing: *a little brother.* Admittedly, I felt some of the same emotional shock as the girls. I had pushed, fought, clawed, and through sheer determination made this moment a possibility, and now here we were, huddled around this boy, *our son*. However, Alexander was able to make all of our shy feelings go away as he gently touched our faces with his small hands, and we in turn touched and hugged him.

Jenny and Svetlana translated for us. We kept asking, "How do you say . . . " about so many things, like his clothes and where we had come from and where we were going.

Most importantly, we wanted to know how to say, "I love you." Svetlana quickly spoke to Alexander, "*Ya lyublyu tebya!*" Then she turned to us, "Just say, 'yellow blue bus.' That's what 'I love you' in Russian sounds like in English."

He did not run, did not hide, did not scream. He wanted us as much as we had wanted him all these months. He was happy, as was I! Like Hannah, I had been given a child, and like Hannah, I cried out in thanksgiving. "Oh Lord, You dragged us through the lowest lows but carried us here, to this moment, to our child."

It didn't take long for Alexander to be ready to go. He was excited to leave this orphanage and go with his family to what he called "Mymerica." He grabbed his Pooh Bear, led us to the window, and insisted, "*Machina, machina, Mymerica!*" while pointing to the car.

But there were a few things we had to do before we rushed out. Lots of pictures were taken, and we changed Alexander's clothes—only I forgot the turtleneck that matched his new pants. And though I had brought him new boots to wear, the mommas insisted that he wear his shoes, not boots. It was immediately clear that the children were used to order, and the mommas were used to doing the ordering.

Though this latest command made no sense to me, we squeezed his feet back into the little red shoes, which they said we could keep.

Jenny asked Alexander to sing for his new family. After a brief moment of shyness, he stood up and sang a song in his small, sweet voice about, as we were later told, "beautiful Russian ladies and handsome Russian men." Apart from the occasional glance to check on Lauren and Jennifer, I couldn't take my eyes off of his little face.

It was no wonder he was a favorite of the mommas; he was not only precious, but he did whatever they asked.

"Now it is your turn," Svetlana announced to Jennifer and Lauren. Both girls were reticent, but I quickly suggested we all sing "My Favorite Things." This song had always been one of our family favorites and seemed appropriate just now: *When the dog bites, when the bee stings, when I'm feeling sad* . . . or overwhelmed and unsure about this very unusual experience. Though I thought our song to be well intentioned but a bit lackluster, it was met with a very kind approval from the mommas. As the applause died down, Svetlana turned to us and asked, "Do you like Sasha? Is this good?"

Jack and I quickly replied, "Yes, of course!"

Svetlana's face beamed as she announced that it was time to celebrate! Unfortunately, the celebratory lunch was not yet ready. In the meantime, we went downstairs to the first room we had entered in to drop off our things. We were encouraged—ordered—to go outside to the playground, which was covered in deep snow.

Alexander was fascinated by the van we had come in, the *machina,* as if he had never laid eyes on one before. He sat on the front seat with Jack and held on to the steering wheel; somehow he knew exactly what to do. After playing for a while on the playground, which the girls loved, the four Americans were cold, and we all went back inside.

Svetlana informed Jack and me that because of the holiday, we could not sign the papers today—it would have to be Tuesday. My heart sank; another delay, the end of which sounded, again, like years away.

We were directed to a large room with a dining table and chairs arranged for our celebratory lunch. I wanted to take pictures but couldn't find my camera. Jenny graciously offered to take me back to the room where we first met Alexander. As we wound through more of the orphanage on the other side of meeting our son, I was braver and looked with more intention into some of the rooms.

What I witnessed was not merely interesting, and not quite depressing, but all rather sad. This time I could see many babies laying in cribs and lots of older children—closer to Alexander's age—just coming in from the outside. They were all bundled up with red cheeks and noses and patiently waited in line to hand in their winter clothing. The mommas busily kept them in line while a lunch for them was prepared. When we didn't find my camera where I thought it might be, we joined the others, and I found it in one of our bags.

At first, I was nervous about lunch. Could we eat it without getting sick, including Alexander? I still really didn't understand celiac disease. I had read about it, but living with a child who actually had it was a different story and concerned me.

As they served the unfamiliar foods, I wondered if my two daughters would balk. As with most young children, Lauren and Jennifer weren't the most adventurous eaters, and the memory of Jennifer throwing up earlier that morning was still very fresh. What if she threw up again? But my fears dissolved with the joy and the excitement of those around me.

The soup that was set before us was some sort of variety of chicken noodle. This was followed by bowls of mashed potatoes, carrots, cabbage, and meat patties. I noticed that Alexander ate with what seemed like a ravenous, hoarding hunger. It didn't seem to matter to him *what* he was eating, as long as he could stuff his little mouth.

With the help of Svetlana, Jack gave the chief doctor of the orphanage the gift of money for Alexander. We also gave them some of the Krispy Kreme trinkets that we had brought from home. With these small details taken care of, it was time for a toast.

Lauren and Jennifer excitedly helped Alexander open a Ring Pop, and they put it on his finger. He quickly caught on to what he was to do from there! Juice was poured for the children, who made some funny, sour faces upon tasting it. Champagne was poured for the adults, and we toasted. By this point in the celebration, we were ready to go, especially Jennifer. Though there were cakes left to eat, blessedly it was agreed that it was time to leave.

The mommas, however, couldn't quite let go. They wanted one last chance to kiss Alexander and to speak with him. While we donned our coats, hats, scarves, and gloves, the whirlwind of mommas laughed and gestured and circulated and oohed and aahed with all kinds of comments, none of which we could understand. It was obvious there was a lot of love there. How could there not be? Alexander was precious and adorable and could stir up joy in just about anyone, which these women had experienced firsthand for almost five years.

Finally, we made it to the *machina,* but we were followed by more than a few mommas with tears running down their cheeks. Alexander, however, was *not* shedding any tears at all—quite the opposite. He was excited and smiling and sat with Jack in the minivan. We waved from the car windows as we drove down the driveway of the orphanage.

We were now a family of five.

13

Taking Care of Business

Jesus, however, called the children to himself and said, "Let the children come to me and do not prevent them."

—Luke 18:16

The girls fell asleep on the drive back into Moscow, and I didn't blame them. Not only were we all physically tired, but we had just experienced the emotional ride of a lifetime. While I was so grateful to have made it this far, this was the beginning of new and different complications. The first step was to legally get Alexander out of Russia—easier said than done. The second would be to get him adjusted to life in America and our family, something I had no time to consider just then. Months and weeks ago when our adoption was in jeopardy, these hurdles were far from my mind, but now that they were imminent, the only thing to do was walk forward in faith.

The most immediate concern was that our son only spoke Russian. We began to compile a list of the most important Russian words from Jenny so that we could communicate with him on our own. We wrote down the English word and then the phonetic spelling of the Russian equivalent. It was quite comical, actually. We needed to have the important ones down, like "eat," "drink," "tinkle," etc.

After paying 30,000 rubles (the equivalent of about 8 U.S. dollars at the time) for a color passport photo of Alexander, we were on to the American Embassy. It was up to the embassy to issue two documents for Alexander that were necessary for our adoption: a passport and a visa. This building, like many others in Moscow at the time, was bland and felt stark and cold. Jack and Jenny went inside while I waited in the van with the children.

While standing in line, Jack was approached by a man who spoke broken English. The man placed a packet of information into my husband's hands and begged him to mail it for him once Jack was back in the United States. Out of kindness or pity, Jack verged on agreeing until Jenny stepped in, returned the envelope, and scolded the man. Jenny vehemently explained to Jack just how dangerous this was for us. This was another sign of just how far from home we had come and another opportunity to be grateful for Jenny and Svetlana.

They maneuvered to a different window and were greeted by a man on the other side. He answered Jenny's questions and gave Jack the paperwork needed for the process. An appointment was made for Thursday morning, six days away.

After another stop for a black and white visa photograph, it was time for dinner. I was worried about my daughters and just how much foreign food they could take.

Jennifer had already thrown up that day, and Lauren wasn't feeling well either. I didn't want our first family meal outside of the orphanage to be one we would want to forget.

Miracle of miracles, the van pulled into a McDonald's! The girls— actually, all of us—were thrilled, a taste of home. No steak or seafood dinner would have tasted better or been more loved and appreciated at that moment.

On our way back to the hotel, we stopped by an outdoor Russian souvenir market. Lauren, Jennifer, and I went in with Jenny. Alexander wasn't interested, so he and Jack waited in the van with the driver.

What a wild, dark scene this market was. The light snow that was falling seemed to cause the few lights mounted here or there to glimmer in the duskiness of the evening that was fast approaching. It would have made an awesome movie set, maybe for *Star Wars* or even *Lord of the Rings*, as the people around us seemed so strange and unfamiliar in their sumptuously warm fur coats, hats, and boots. From the dark clothing they were wearing to the colorful folk art they were offering, I was reminded that I was very far from home; maybe I had even landed in an imaginary land. I was in a daze.

Especially captivating were the Russian nesting dolls that were featured in dozens of stalls. They were enticingly beautiful and came in so many different sizes, shapes, and bright colors. They seemed to sparkle in the midst of so much darkness. Jenny haggled with the vendors for better prices. I purchased quite a few of these new and enigmatic treasures.

Meanwhile, back in the car, Jack noticed that Alexander began to hold his stomach and whimper. He started speaking to the driver, and Jack could not understand what he was saying. The driver did his best to explain to Jack, and finally, after some back and forth, Jack finally grasped the idea: Alexander needed to go to the bathroom. But where? Jack remembered the words of warning from the Barkers about finding a hotel, but there was no hotel around here. The three got out of the van, and the driver vaguely pointed down some stairs.

Jack looked where he pointed in disbelief and concern.

Jack and Alexander descended into a subway-like place below ground that was very cold, very damp, and very dirty—and probably very unsafe. The structure was built of concrete blocks that had once been painted but were now discolored and decrepit. The row of metal stalls that awaited them below seemed ominous to Jack, but he had to pick one and help Alexander use it.

Alexander had a bad case of diarrhea, but the only toilet paper available was torn pages from a few magazines and books that were hanging on a hook on the back of the stall door. Blessedly, I missed out on this experience, and, thank God, everyone made it back to the van safely. When we were warned to bring toilet paper to Russia, we didn't think we would need to bring it everywhere we went. Needless to say, Jack has never taken toilet paper for granted again.

Now back to the Hotel Ukraine for our first night together as a family.

At first Alexander was afraid of the bathtub, until he saw his sisters get in. He hopped in after them and did not want to get out. When we finally got all three out and dressed, Alexander settled into bed next to his dad. But he was restless and too excited to sleep, and understandably so. Repeatedly, he would sit up and roll over and feel our faces. Despite how close we had already grown, we were still speaking two different languages.

"*Pee-sat*," Alexander said.

Jack checked the list of words we had compiled with Jenny. Jack had written this word down to mean "drink" or "thirsty," so he got him a glass of water.

Alexander took a sip, but then repeated, "*Pee-sat.*"

Again, Jack offered the glass of water, and again Alexander took a sip.

"*Pee-sat,*" Alexander said again.

This cycle repeated itself several more times until Jack finally took Alexander to the bathroom, hoping this would solve the problem. It did. Jack realized that "*peet*" was "drink," but "*pee-sat*" was "tinkle."

At long last, we settled down to get some much-needed sleep.

The following morning, we went to visit a Russian hospital, which had a lot in common with the orphanage—both had been poorly cared for, almost neglected. Though the building was depressing and dilapidated, the people inside were kind and helpful. We also met two other American couples hoping to adopt like we were and, like us, were probably just trying to do everything in their power to bring their children home.

Jack, Jenny, Alexander, and I were ushered into a room that was small and sparsely furnished. Jennifer and Lauren waited in a room next to ours, and Jack and I took turns checking on them.

Eventually two doctors entered. The first was a young man and a pediatrician-in-training, who served as our translator. Alexander's primary pediatrician was an older, rather unkempt Russian woman. She was reminiscent of the mommas at the orphanage—and just as good with Alexander. She offered him an orange Tic Tac if he would listen to her and do what she asked.

She spoke continually while the young man translated as quickly as he could. They told us many things, most of which we knew already, like that his size and weight were low for his age. He had already had chicken pox, she said, was lactose intolerant, and had celiac disease. I listened respectfully to what both doctors had to say, but I looked forward to getting Alexander before a doctor back in the States.

Upon our return to the Hotel Ukraine, we visited another restaurant on the third floor, which was much different than the one where we dined on our first night. This one was beautifully decorated, almost fancy, and had American music playing in the background.

It was difficult and a bit awkward that we spoke no Russian, unlike our son, who could communicate easily with the waitresses. They liked Alexander, they liked that we were American, and they seemed to approve of what we were doing—at least we hoped so. However, like so many of the people we encountered, we wondered what they were truly thinking. What was it like to have foreigners come into your city, adopt one of your children, and bring him back to their country?

Pushing these concerns aside, Jack and I struggled to figure out what to feed Alexander, given that everyone had told us he could not eat gluten or dairy. Alexander, on the other hand, was excited to eat anything and everything, as if he had not eaten in a while. Overall, the food was much more to our liking, making the $110 bill worth it in the end.

This was to be our "big" meal for the day as we were going out later with Jenny on what we were told was an exciting excursion. It would be a late evening—especially for the children. We were instructed to "rest" this afternoon, or at least be quiet and "chill" so we would all be ready for what the Victoria Tourist House had planned for us. I had brought some simple art supplies and note cards for a time like this, hoping the girls could use markers and paint images of the places and people they had observed on this trip of a lifetime. Perhaps they could later share these pictures with their friends and teachers once we were back home. *Home* ... that sounded really nice just then—and very far away.

14

A God of Gifts

All good giving and every perfect gift is from above,
coming down from the Father of lights.

—James 1:17

At five o'clock that evening, Jenny came in the van to take us out on what would be our first excursion as tourists since our arrival. Though we knew we were going to the ballet, we were not told exactly what we were going to see, and we didn't ask. Jenny instructed us to dress nicely, but despite the twelve suitcases we had brought with us, fancy clothing had not been put into any of them. So Jack and I wore our best jeans, and the girls wore their best travel outfits. Alexander, being too young for the ballet, would be with Svetlana at her home with Jenny there to help keep an eye as well.

To our pleasant surprise, we were dropped off at the famous Bolshoi Theatre. Built in the nineteenth century, the Bolshoi was home to world-class performances of its ballet and orchestra. After speaking for a while outside in the cold with a couple from Connecticut, the doors finally opened at 6:15 p.m., and the four of us rushed in with a crowd of others. The only problem was that we had no idea where to go. We showed our tickets to the attendant, who pointed us up the stairs. When we got upstairs, we showed our tickets to the attendant, who pointed us back downstairs.

We were so confused—and language deficient. Only after stopping and watching the crowds for a minute did we realize that we were first supposed to check our coats.

This seemed to be very important. I guess "order" was a characteristic of Russia itself, not just for the mommas in the orphanage. As with many cultures, the Russians had certain formalities within their culture that needed to be observed, and we were happy to do so.

We had just enough time to check out the refreshments, which were in a pretty room with two tables. There were pastries, open-faced sandwiches with caviar, champagne, and fruit juice, all of which looked delicious. The four of us shared two pastries and both girls had some juice. Jack and I took advantage of the champagne!

Finally, we found our seats, and I was able to take in the beauty of the room. Every detail, it seemed, was trimmed in gold. Burgundy box seating was majestically stacked in five layers and surrounded the lower seats. Above my head, crystal chandeliers were beautifully hung. Then the lights faded, and the curtains opened; it was time for the show to begin.

The conductor stood before the crowd to a light applause. He faced his orchestra and lifted his baton. As the violinists drew their bows across the strings, it did not take long for us to recognize the music from this short prelude played prior to the curtains opening. It was *The Nutcracker.*

What a blessing from God, Who had already shown me He was a God of gifts. Now I knew Him to be the God of surprises and gifts on top of gifts, and I cried tears of joy and gratitude as the curtains were drawn.

God our Father gave us such a special gift in this *Nutcracker* ballet. In the bathroom with my mother-in-law's holy card, I had given up looking for signs from God in exchange for faith, but here I felt so strongly the affirming peace of God that we were on the right track, we were where He wanted us to be, doing what He desired us to do. Our little family loved this story—it was a family tradition, and here we were in the land where it was created. Lauren and Jennifer were smiling from ear to ear.

The lights gave the effect of falling snow as an endless sequence of dancers tiptoed onto the scene from stage right. But what also made this performance so amazing was the stark differences when compared to the American version we had attended only a month before. There were no children in the Russian *Nutcracker*; all the dancers were adults. The Nutcracker was a real person, and Godpapa Drosselmeyer carried him in and put him under the tree (which grew, just as ours did back home!). Only the parents danced, and they did so with beer steins in hand. Marie, played by a beautiful ballerina, did not kill the Mouse King with her shoe; he just ran away. At the end of the first half, the Nutcracker became a handsome prince.

During intermission, we were approached by a Russian woman who must have heard us talking.

"You are Americans?" she asked. "Yes," we replied.

She motioned at us with her camera and asked repeatedly, "Yes? Yes? Yes?"

Although we were unsure exactly *why* she wanted our picture, we obligingly agreed. The four of us looked at her and smiled as she snapped the camera. We felt famous—just because we were Americans.

The second half opened under a Christmas tree. Marie was now the Sugar Plum Fairy, and as the story progressed, we realized another difference—this was a love story. Marie and the Prince danced together across the stage. I couldn't help thinking of Alexander, my little prince, whom I had fallen in love with at first sight. You could feel the audience falling in love with their Prince, and the show culminated in a wedding at the end.

"Bravo! Bravo!" the audience belted over their own raucous applause. The ovations and calls to bring Marie and the Prince back out rolled over again and again.

This, I knew, would be a memory—and a gift—that I would treasure forever.

As I have mentioned, our Russian contacts were travel agents—and they were *excellent* travel agents. As one of the first American families to adopt from Russia, we were also blessed to be among the first Americans to experience everything Svetlana and her company could do for visitors. If we were merely tourists, we would have been pleased, but because we were a new family looking to bond, we were elated and overjoyed. On Sunday, the experience continued as Jenny took us to Kolomenskoye Park to see traditional folk dancing and experience a *troika* (sleigh) ride.

At the park we looked longingly at the fur boots and coats and the leather gloves that the Russians were wearing. We had brought the best we could find in the States, but, despite these efforts, we didn't have the right socks or gloves. Nevertheless, we played in the snow as the people all around us enjoyed themselves skiing and sledding. Our numb toes and icy fingers were worth it.

Later, aboard the sleigh, I imagined myself in *The Nutcracker*. We—Jack, myself, and our three children—were all on our way to a Christmas party to meet Godpapa Drosselmeyer. Lauren,

Jennifer, and Alexander were bonding so quickly and seamlessly; it was a magical experience, not to mention fun and beautiful.

For dinner, Jenny took us to a special Russian restaurant. Once inside, we were led downstairs to a small intimate room with a table just for our group. We indulged in several courses and were warmed by delicious vodka. No wonder it is so treasured here! We were stuffed, but after a quick rest at the hotel, it was on to the Russian Circus.

I am sure that Alexander had never seen anything like it. Though the children at the orphanage went out to play and occasionally had a Christmas outing, it was not likely that they ever attended shows like the Russian Circus.

After checking our coats—no confusion this time!—Jenny's handsome friend Andre met us at our seats. We learned that he was studying to be a physician. In the former Soviet system, physicians were one of the lowest paid and least valued careers, which might partially explain why there were many misdiagnoses of orphan children. However, Andre didn't seem to mind things like pay; he genuinely wanted to take care of people.

As our children had bonded over candy and sleigh rides, here too they could just enjoy being children. Acrobats leaped and spun around the ring as different clowns and figures would wander into their midst from a large set of stairs to our left. The cactus and bee clowns were, hands down, our favorites. The robot made the children laugh as he laboriously descended one stair at a time. Father Christmas—or perhaps it was Father Frost, seeing as he was dressed in a bluish-gray robe—waltzed in as well, to the delight of the crowd. He was similar to Santa Claus, but he was more slender and sported a much longer beard.

The next morning was the ninth of January. We made the mistake of sleeping in until nine o'clock, so we rushed to make it to breakfast. I'm not sure why, since the breakfasts at the hotel were not particularly delicious, but Jack and I did crave some coffee.

Jenny called to say that their minivan had broken down. It would be lunchtime before they could come and get us. Since we were dressed and ready to go (and caffeinated), we went out to play in the snow. Just in front of our hotel was the large, imposing statue that chilled us upon arrival at the hotel a few nights before. However, we had learned from our travel agents that he was not Lenin or Stalin, but rather a Ukrainian poet, artist, and political figure named Taras Shevchenko.

Shevchenko was also an orphan, having lost both parents at a young age. In his poem "I Was Thirteen," he speaks of a girl who, upon hearing his cries, comes to wipe his tears and kiss his face. While a political prisoner in Russia, he longed for his Ukrainian homeland. However, he died the day after his forty-seventh birthday in St. Petersburg with his dream of returning to Ukraine left unfulfilled.

In a way, we were doing for Alexander what Shevchenko had dreamed for himself. Like the girl in Shevchenko's poem, we had come for Alexander, to wipe away his tears, kiss his little face, and bring him home. And in hindsight, perhaps God had been pursuing me all that time, too, desiring *me* just as I was desiring and pursuing another child. He was using this journey to bring me on another one—a journey deeper into His own heart. He saw my tears and gently brushed them aside, turning my sorrow into faith and my faith into joy.

He longs to bring all of us home to Himself—even the broken, hurting, and hungering parts of us—just as I longed and was working so hard to take Alexander home with me. There is no substitute for God, and there is no wound or crack that He does not desire to enter into and heal.

We played and sledded in Shevchenko's shadow for quite a while. It was fun to just relax, play, and wander around—just the five of us. If we could just make it back to North Carolina, this was what it would be like from now on.

Before Jenny arrived, Beth Lyndon, our friend who was also trying to adopt and who had first mentioned Alexander, called. It was so good to talk with someone from home. She was in awe that in such a short time we were speaking with such wisdom and knowledge about the process of adoption in Russia.

But isn't that what happens when life occurs and you're suddenly in the middle of what you have dreamed of and planned for so long? However, it turned out to be an afternoon of ups and downs. Perhaps, the pace of our travels was beginning to catch up with us.

Our first stop was another, yet smaller and more intimate, souvenir market, where Jenny helped us yet again to haggle with the vendors. The entire market floor was a sheet of ice, and in the middle of shopping, Jennifer slipped and fell, which put a damper on things. Alexander wasn't interested in anything the market had to offer. On the long car ride back into town, Lauren got carsick.

What we needed was a great dinner, but the thought of another plate of mystery meat or borscht soup made me worried for the children. To my delight, Jenny asked the driver to drop us off at Pizza Hut!

In the final years of the Soviet Union, American fast-food retailers were gradually allowed to open up locations in Russia, with McDonald's being the first in 1990. Other chains soon followed, including Burger King, KFC, Starbucks, and—one of our children's favorites—Pizza Hut.

As the five of us excitedly approached the door, a young soldier wielding a rather large gun stopped us at the door.

"*Nyet dostupnykh stolov*," he said quite seriously, with a hand on his gun.

Though Alexander probably understood what he was saying, there was no way for him to translate. We motioned that we wanted to enter the restaurant to eat.

"*Nyet dostupnykh stolov*!" he forcefully repeated while stepping in front of us.

Jack and I looked at each other with concern. Was something wrong? Were we in trouble? Why was he gripping his gun so tightly?

Another young man was leaving the restaurant, and I asked him if he spoke English. He did, and he translated for us. The young soldier with the gun was trying to tell us to wait—there was no table available!

A bit cranky and over the top, if you ask me.

15

Mymerica

Return home and recount what God has done for you.

—Luke 8:39

That Tuesday we had to be up and out early. Our first stop was to buy candy for the staff at the orphanage—there was a bit of unfinished business we had to take care of there.

Alexander and the other orphans, as I mentioned, were trained —or hardened—to never cry. As we were driving back into Podolsk, Alexander must have recognized where we were going. Despite Jenny's best effort to explain and reassure, Alexander grew more upset and concerned the closer we got to the orphanage. Perhaps in his mind, these few days with us were just another school outing or a dream to be cut short.

This time I was stronger emotionally and mentally, and though Alexander needed me then and there, I was still better able to take a look at the little town of Podolsk—and realized that it was rather depressing. Even the layer of snow, which had enlivened our hearts elsewhere, looked dirty in this small, industrial city.

When we arrived at the orphanage, Jack, Jenny, and Alexander went inside, while the girls and I remained in the van. There Jenny retrieved Alexander's original birth certificate. At the first sight of one of the mommas, Alexander cried. We could only guess that he thought he was going to have to stay. Jack held him close and reassured him as best he could.

The principal of the orphanage, still topped off by her tall, white hat, joined our little group and drove with us to another location to obtain Alexander's "Letter of Abandonment." At this stop, the principal met with another Russian woman while the five of us plus Jenny waited in the van. We waited about fifteen to twenty minutes as these ladies "did their thing," as Jenny explained and rolled her eyes in obvious disgust. Although they were getting the Russian paperwork done, Jenny didn't seem to be impressed with this part of the process, but her funny faces and comments made Jack and me chuckle.

After obtaining the letter, we had to drop the principal back off at the orphanage. As we drove down the driveway for the second time that day, Alexander cried yet again. He simply could not understand that we weren't going to abandon him there and leave him alone. Perhaps, when we pulled away for the third time, the reality of the permanence of his new family was beginning to sink in.

The principal was very gracious to us. She went into the orphanage and brought out some sandwiches, which, though unappealing to us, pleased Alexander. She also gave us some "medicine" for Alexander's tummy issues. Being more than a bit skeptical, I never gave it to him.

Another step forward. Oh, how many steps there were to climb on this mountain! We had climbed, then fallen, then climbed and fallen again, and we continued climbing.

As we later drove here and there around greater Moscow in our van, Jenny shared many things with us that were very meaningful and helped us understand all that was going on. She said that the children in orphanages were told that their parents would come back for them one day. And now here was Alexander, whose tears had been stifled and suppressed for so long, and yet now he was willing to let them out, to let us see them. We hoped this was a sign that Alexander didn't merely see us as random adults or guardians, but truly as his parents.

At this point I believe God was giving us another gift—perseverance—to be able to continue on this path we had chosen and that He desired us to take so that He could give us the gift we longed for: *our son.*

At this point in our journey, I felt like I was living out another special moment from *The Sound of Music*, which (if you haven't picked up on this already) is one of my favorite movies of all time. Nearing the climax of the story, the Reverend Mother says to Maria, "You must live the life you were born to live," and then Reverend Mother begins to sing the song, "Climb Ev'ry Mountain."

We were only days away from bringing our son home. Home to Mymerica and home to our house; home to our family traditions and home to our way of life. Jack and I felt so close to completing what God was calling us to do, thus fulfilling our dream of another child. We could imagine what the "top"—the completion of our climb—would feel like, but we still had a ways to go.

For now, it was back to Moscow, where our dreams and desires were next in the hands of the Moscow Center of Adoptions.

Alexander was scared of the dog that met us at the door of the Victoria Tourist House, where we were to eat lunch before heading to the Moscow Center of Adoptions. Having spent most of his life walking in and around the orphanage, he had probably only ever encountered the wild dogs we had seen earlier on our drive through Podolsk. I hoped that our own dog, Sam, could help him to overcome this fear.

After using the bathroom—with normal toilet paper—we took a tour of the agency, then sat down for lunch. While we ate, Svetlana and another of her employees insisted we were "heroes" for what we were doing. That was helpful and gratifying to hear, especially from two Russian citizens. We also learned from Svetlana that Jenny and her "friend" Andre were much more than friends. In fact, they were discussing marriage!

When the lunch was finished, and while Alexander sang for all the ladies, we met with Svetlana in her office to discuss the next step. We needed to present a gift to the Moscow Center of Adoptions, and what they needed was a copier. Svetlana showed us a brand-new copier still in the box that she had purchased as part of our $10,000 fee. A little strange, but yet again, we did what we were told.

After a short drive, we arrived at the Moscow Center of Adoptions—one more mile marker along our Russian adoption journey. One more gift to give as a "thank you" for our son. One more check off the list, but this one caused me the greatest concern so far.

Svetlana, Jack, and I went inside the nondescript building while Jenny stayed in the van with the children. This was the first and only time that Jack and I had left the children behind somewhere in Russia—and I was anxious.

Once inside, we had to step onto a very tiny and very old Russian elevator with a heavy copy machine in a large, brown box. There wasn't enough room for the door to close until we worked together to hoist the machine over our heads. The resulting claustrophobia only added to my anxiety. Thankfully Jack saw the concern—mixed with some fear—on my face and began to be a little silly. This caused Svetlana to start giggling, and by the time the door finally opened, they were in hysterics, and I was at least smiling.

"Let's get this done and get back to the van" was what my mind was focused on.

The director of the Moscow Center of Adoptions was a slender, older woman with white hair. In fact, despite the intimidating title, she was not to be feared; she and Svetlana were friends. Looking around her office, Jack and I saw on various bulletin boards hanging on the walls the pictures of all the children she had helped to place.

After we presented our gift, she went to her cabinet, pulled out a small gold medal on a blue silk ribbon, and placed it around my neck. She kissed me on both cheeks, and said, "Congratulations on being a new mother." I was so touched and astounded by this that I wanted to cry, but I held it in. All I really wanted to do was get back to that van.

But this was all so unbelievable, like something out of a movie: my movie. Another lady in this office called with news concerning Alexander's passport, which was ready! Praise God! We picked it up on the way back to the van and celebrated with another dinner at McDonald's.

That night at the hotel, I woke up in a sweat and a panic, as if awaking from a nightmare. All my fears and concerns were racing through my brain: What if I had come out of the building where the director of adoptions had her office, and the white van was gone? And my children with it? Gone into the dark night of Moscow. It was years before I could let go of that nightmare and all the other "what-ifs" that came along with it.

The next morning, it came as no shock that our three children didn't care much for touring Red Square. Not only was the tour a bit long, but it was a snowy, cold day in Moscow. The tour was not to be missed though, since we would be seeing the Dormition Cathedral and St. Basil's Cathedral. Though my suspicions of Russia itself were not eased by being so close to the infamous Kremlin, many of my anxieties had been alleviated by so many of the lovely "locals" we had interacted with.

Not least of these was Svetlana, who informed us later that afternoon that she needed to leave the country immediately for Budapest, where her ninety-five-year-old mother was ill. She apologized wholeheartedly for missing Lauren's tenth birthday the next day, but she did bring gifts. Lauren opened a box with a stuffed penguin inside, and, thankfully, the next gift was a big box of chocolates (someone must have shared that Lauren was a bit of a chocoholic). Alexander and Jennifer weren't left out and opened gifts of their own. Svetlana presented Jack and I with a tape of a famous Russian singer whom we had never heard of, but we were being taught by our new Russian friends that it was the gesture—the thought—that mattered.

After opening the gifts we had brought for her and her husband, Svetlana shared her exciting news: Andre and Jenny were engaged! After all that these few special people had done for us, it was like hearing that a relative had been proposed to. This also explained the sadness that would eventually overshadow our heartfelt goodbye.

Later that day, as we waited for dinner at a hotel restaurant, we heard a band playing in a nearby room. Leaving Jack and Lauren behind, I grabbed Jennifer and Alexander by the hand as we skipped together into the room, where we danced. While the Russian music filled our ears as we twirled and laughed together, I couldn't help but think that this might be one of Alexander's last experiences of Russian culture, of the land in which he was born. How he would adapt to America, and how quickly, was a worry still unresolved. We still had to get home to find out.

I awoke with a start. This was it, the day of our exit interview. Just as in the States, our folks in Russia had to look over our paperwork, make sure we had jumped through all the required hoops, and then give us their stamp of approval for us to leave and go home.

Our appointment at the embassy was set for 9:15 a.m. The final hurdle! We missed our way of life, we missed our dog and cat, and we even missed our currently under-renovation house.

I was terrified, and Jack was too. Just how many times had we been disappointed by an arm of the government in this process? What if the person responsible for these final papers was in a bad mood today, was just plain mean spirited, or made a careless mistake? If the American government could issue an *intent to deny* for so small a reason, then what was the Russian government capable of?

I pushed those anxieties to the side, mostly for the sake of Lauren. We did not want her to feel like we had forgotten about her birthday just because we were in a cramped hotel room on the other side of the world. She was so positive, despite the circumstances. We arranged breakfast in bed, consisting mostly of the various snacks we had packed in our suitcase, and sang "Happy Birthday." Alexander knew none of the words but was happy to participate anyway.

When we arrived at the American Embassy, there was a long line of Russians waiting (and hoping) to receive their visas to the United States. We went around them and climbed the stairs to the same room Jack had entered on our first visit there. This time we were surrounded by many other Americans waiting (and hoping) to adopt Russian children. Of course, I knew people back home who had been through this process, but at the sight of this crowded room, I knew beyond a shadow of a doubt that what we were trying to do was not at all crazy, but rather loving and good and natural—a sharing in the love of our Heavenly Father, whose greatest desire is to bring us home to Himself.

At the sound of our name, Jack and I approached the window where we were sort of greeted—but really just acknowledged—by a nice-looking young man with dark brown hair. Being that he at least on some level stood between us and our son, we gave it our best shot to befriend him. We even told him our connection to Krispy Kreme Doughnuts and slipped him some Krispy Kreme souvenirs, trying to make him smile.

He blandly handed us more forms to fill out and asked for Alexander's passport. We were told to wait in chairs lining the walls. Sitting there I prayed silently, *Please Lord, let this be done! You have heard my cries and brought me this far! Move some hearts on our behalf!*

An hour later, our names were called, and we anxiously approached the window. My heart sank, as all he wanted was to ask a few more questions and for $200 cash. More waiting, more praying.

Soon thereafter we were approached by a lady with red hair and glasses who said she was there to help us. We had a good laugh about Krispy Kreme; it was obvious she was a fan. She lamented that she hadn't had a really good doughnut in more than a year and a half, and we replied that we wished we had one to give her.

After a bit more back and forth, she asked us to come back at five o'clock for Alexander's visa. Back in the van, Jenny said that the red-haired lady was never that kind and even had a reputation for being rude.

So, yet another testimony to the power of the doughnut—and prayer.

Jenny dropped us back at the hotel for a bit, and I decided to be brave and go out *by myself* and do a little more shopping. Being out on my own shows how far I had come: from being a frightened basket case when we first arrived in Russia to now a casual tourist out looking for souvenirs. As I walked along window shopping, the beautiful snow fell—making everything more peaceful and lovely—and I reflected on how far we had come. Had I really, through the ups and downs, doubted God and His Providence? Now, there was a beautiful boy calling me "mama." In a few hours, God willing, Jack and I would have his visa in hand, and we—and our three children—would be on our way home.

But first, it was on to an American hotel, the Radisson, to celebrate Lauren's birthday with an early dinner. This hotel, more than any other place in Moscow, reminded us of home. Too bad we could not have stayed here during our trip, but we had been given no say in the matter. The decor was familiar, and the food was a bit more "normal"—even the children said so. Lauren was surprised when a waiter brought out a cake with ten candles, and then she happily opened her gifts. She wasn't the only one, though; we also presented Jenny with a gift, and, from her very pretty smile, she seemed pleased.

After a couple of stops, it was back to the American Embassy. We arrived at 5:10 p.m.—a few minutes late—and I was once again nervous and scared. Whether or not we all went home tomorrow was in these people's hands. What if they had access to my fingerprints? What if they somehow knew of the original intent to deny issued by the INS?

Ours was the first name called, and I bravely, yet hopefully, approached the window. A different man with a round face was holding Alexander's visa there in his hand. He lectured me with stern instructions for what seemed like a lifetime about what to do and not to do with the visa. I wanted to shout, "Hurry up and give it to me!" but instead I patiently listened and nodded. At that moment, I would have promised to do just about anything he said.

He slipped it under the glass, and I scooped it up. It was like gold in my hands.

Victory! Thank You, God! Jenny congratulated and hugged us. Jack and I waved goodbye to the other couples, then we practically galloped down the stairs with our three children in tow and outside into the snow. Hurrah! We headed "home" to the hotel, but soon it would be *home* to America, to "Mymerica."

But not before a celebratory glass of wine.

As we were driven to the airport in the dark of the early morning, the streets of Moscow seemed different than they had at our arrival. Was it simply that the sun had not risen, or that I had changed over the past week, or both? Had we brought with us a charitable spirit that we were now leaving behind? Or, was a part of me *grateful* to God for using this place, despite its turbulent recent history, to bring my son—a child who had grown in my heart if not in my womb—into my arms and claim him as my own? To face incredible obstacles, not the least of which was my own fear, I had discovered so much about myself and my God in the process!

Jenny accompanied us the entire way: from handing over our bags, to having our tickets confirmed and printed, and finally having our passports checked. Realizing this was goodbye, there were tears in her eyes. She knew that the future was bright for us, for our son, and we hoped the same was true for her and Andre.

She picked up Alexander and told him in Russian just how lucky he was to be going to America, his *Mymerica*. After she translated for us what she had said and Alexander's responses, Jenny hugged each of us one last time, and we hugged her. We walked on, but I turned and waved and called out, "yellow blue bus!" With her most beautiful smile, Jenny responded, "I love you too!"

Despite his excitement at leaving the orphanage in our "*machina*," Alexander was a bit frightened as we boarded the airplane and throughout our long flight to the United States. Because of the language barrier, it was hard to explain what was happening and to reassure him. Several bilingual stewardesses helped us as best they could, all of whom were touched by the story of our adoption. They even made Alexander a detailed map of his flight path from Russia to the United States, and they all signed it.

Our landing in Charlotte was made better when we learned that Mac had arranged for the Krispy Kreme plane to take us home to Winston-Salem. What an unexpected blessing. Thank you, Mac. It had been a very emotional and mind-blowing ten days, but we did it. We climbed our mountain and came down the other side, safe and sound. *Thank You, God! Thank you, thank you, Lovely Lady Dressed in Blue!*

16

Child of Mine

The child is the beauty of God present in the world, that greatest gift to a family.

—St. Teresa of Calcutta

Alexander came into our family, and our lives became even busier. But through it all, God was drawing us ever closer to Him. Holiness is a process, a journey that takes us closer and closer to God. I had experienced an extraordinary encounter with grace through Our Blessed Mother's intercession and came to understand that she was all the time leading me to *her* Son, as well as Jack and I to our own.

When God places something—a wish, a desire, *His will*—on your heart and through perseverance and God's grace you respond, you're actually growing in holiness, sometimes without even realizing it. Through His gift of grace, which is an *unmerited gift of divine favor,* God was changing our hearts as well as our lives, drawing us ever closer to Himself.

As soon as we returned home, I began work on the adoption announcement that I had promised to send out in gratitude to Our Blessed Mother. Jack took a black-and-white close-up photo of our three children, and I put together the text.

The very special prayer, *Lovely Lady Dressed in Blue,* would be on the inside, as I had promised. I have since learned that this prayer was written in 1926 by Mary Dixon Thayer. When Ven. Archbishop Fulton J. Sheen fell in love with it, he promoted it, and because of his intense devotion to Our Blessed Mother, he ended many of his television shows and presentations by reciting it. I would bet my sweet and holy mother-in-law watched some of his shows and so knew and loved this prayer as well. Perhaps that is why she shared it with me that day when I was in such desperate need.

I wish I had asked her more about this prayer and why she gave it to me that fateful day *when I had the chance.*

On the back of our adoption announcement, I added the song "Child of Mine" by Carole King, which best expressed what I was trying to say as my own words seemed to fail me. This song, written much like a poem, sounded like a mother speaking to her child, reminding him that although the circumstances in which he had been born might not have been ideal, he could make his dreams come true by the way he lived his life—and by his beautiful smile. The refrain, by itself, expressed so much of what was on my heart, "Oh, yes, sweet darling/ So glad you are a child of mine."

So many friends and family welcomed us home with presents and food.

A friend of mine asked me, "Well, how much weight did you lose?"

I really hadn't thought about it, but she was right. We had all lost a bit of weight in Russia, so any food was welcome. It wasn't that there was a lack of food in Russia, but rather there was a deficit of the snacks we were used to eating here at home. As a Communist country for so many years, Russia's economy had been stifled, which limited the availability of so many fun and yummy products like those we are blessed with in the United States.

Though everyone was eager to offer us home-cooked meals and treats, they were even more eager to meet Alexander. One of our neighbors made an observation that has stayed with me these past twenty-five years. Trying to be funny, she commented, "Alexander went from zero to Disney World in one day!"

We all laughed when she said it, but she was right. What a miracle—to travel from a difficult situation with little hope to one of stability and love, from an orphanage to a home with parents and siblings (and a dog and a cat), from an uncertain future to one bright with promise.

Through his adoption, Alexander was now an equal member of our family, just as we, through our baptism, are all equal members of God's family. We traveled to the ends of the earth to claim a child, the child God had desired for us and whom I claimed for my own, just as God claims each one of us as His own *adopted and beloved* child.

It was good to be home, even though ours was still a bit topsy-turvy due to the renovation. But it didn't matter to us anymore. We had all experienced a cultural wake-up call and came back from ten days in Russia with a renewed gratitude for all of life's blessings, great and small. There were so many simple pleasures that we had previously taken for granted, and Alexander now gave witness to the fact that these small blessings were *special*, such as a warm bath, a toothbrush, and a full tummy, just to name a few.

We had worked so hard to make Alexander's room cute, fun, and happy, with lots of primary colors and stuffed animals. When we showed it to him, he liked everything, but he wanted to see where Lauren and Jennifer were sleeping. When we tried to have him sleep in his own bed in his own room, he cried. He would have none of it. He wanted to sleep with his sisters, which he did for quite a while.

Little did I know the comedic result of this sleeping dilemma.

Thankfully, many of the worries I could have had before the meeting in Hickory, before the applications and meetings, and before physically departing for Russia never fully registered with me. The biggest concern I now faced was the language barrier and the catch-up Alexander would need regarding school and overall fitting in. Russian is a difficult language to learn, but so is English. Perhaps because children are so open and pliable, he gave it his best and learned quickly—and I was proud of him for it.

Some English phrases and concepts Alexander grasped more quickly than others, and he used them prolifically, often to my dismay. For example, Alexander loved to tell people that he was going to marry them—and he didn't limit this statement to just girls his age. He would announce this to women who were already married, like his preschool teacher, who would point to her husband and reply, "Well, you have to talk to *him* about that!" He even proposed to one of the nuns at his school, Sr. Emma.

One of Alexander's favorite questions was, "Who do you sleep with?" It was very important to him who *he* slept with: at first his sisters and later on his own in his own bedroom. Alexander and I would be in the grocery store, and as we would pull up to another shopper, he would loudly and intently ask, "Who do *you* sleep with?"

He was very serious about this question and very interested in the other person's answer. Without fail, the stranger would look at me then usually (but not always) smile graciously and answer his question.

In the early days of this game, I would be caught by surprise, red-faced and stuttering. But as I came to expect this behavior from him, I would laugh and give a simple explanation, and eventually we would all three end up at least smiling, if not chuckling.

The more English he learned, the more questions he was able to ask and the more answers I needed to have. Being adopted at almost five years old, of course, he remembered some things, but he had a limited grasp or understanding of what had actually happened earlier in his young life.

Two questions that haunted us were why he had been born "somewhere else," and why did we have to go and get him? Being so young, he didn't fully understand exactly where babies came from, so for a long time I would bravely explain that the "stork" had just messed up and taken him way off course. Then we had to get on a plane, go find him, and bring him home.

I believe I had also clung to this make-believe story in my own heart. I too wished the stork had just messed up. It was such an easier and less complicated reality. Now I realize that far from being a "mistake," God's plan for us had been far better than any fairy tale we could possibly have created for ourselves.

I learned that another difficulty that comes with learning a new language is adapting to a culture's idioms and expressions. Alexander picked up on many of them, but some took a bit more time. During gymnastics class, which Alexander loved attending, he would copy the other children as they played and did gymnastics moves. One day he was following and copying a little girl in the class.

Finally, she turned and said to him with a bit of irritation, "You are a copycat!"

Alexander looked at her, pondered for a few seconds, and replied very matter-of-factly, "Well, you are a copy dog."

Seeing that he had come to love dogs since landing in America, especially his own dog, Sam, I think he thought he was offering a compliment.

As his mom, I just thought it was clever.

When we were going through the home study, Jack and I were asked by both Marie and Catherine if we were going to change Alexander's birth year. We were both surprised and asked, "Why on earth would we do that?" Their answers were similar: because adopted children, especially if they came with a different language, were often behind their peers and needed a little "help" to catch up.

I was distressed at the thought of changing such an important milestone as our son's actual day of birth. It seemed like we would be lying to him and to the world. We are all born on a specific day, and we celebrate that day throughout our lives. To change such a special and important day was very unsettling.

But now that we were faced with placing Alexander in school and fitting him into a new life in a new country, we realized why many parents *did* change their child's birthday—at least their birth year. In the years that followed, I sometimes regretted our decision, as Alexander worked and struggled to catch up to his peers. But I do love and honor his actual birth date, and he does too.

Alexander did end up attending St. Leo the Great Catholic School, and we were grateful for their openness and support. The teachers there had many funny stories in the early months with him. One of the funniest came from his preschool teacher, Mrs. Frazell.

She told of being at circle time with her preschool class. She liked to keep Alexander next to her to "keep an eye on him," which was probably smart—especially after he proposed to her. One day while reading a story to the class, she felt a small hand running up and down her thigh, on top of her pantyhose. For a few minutes, she was unable to move and unsure how to handle this situation, as it had never occurred before.

She managed to control the hand, finish circle time, and then ask Alexander what was going on. As it turned out, he was fascinated with pantyhose, having never seen them before. Thankfully, Mrs. Frazell was very lighthearted and forgiving.

To my dismay, however, he managed to run his hand along many a lady's leg.

Humility, humility, humility.

With our lives—and our home—back in some sense of order, we knew we needed to have Alexander baptized. He was our son, but he needed to be *adopted* as God's son as well.

At His own baptism in the Jordan, Jesus received a special outpouring of the Holy Spirit, Who descended in the form of a dove, and which prefigured our own Christian Baptism. A heavenly voice proclaimed, "You are my beloved Son; with you I am well pleased" (Mark 1:11).

Of course Alexander was *our* beloved son, and of course God loved him, but he too needed to receive the precious gift of the Holy Spirit and be born into the holy body of the Church, the people of Christ. Fr. Jim Solari, our pastor at St. Leo the Great Catholic Church, baptized Alexander on October 22, 1995.

Since it is usually babies who are baptized, it was very heartwarming to watch a little boy receive baptism, as young children still possess the gift of *wonder.* You could see on his sweet and innocent face that Alexander was intrigued with all that was happening to him during the baptismal ceremony. As Alexander lay relaxed in Jack's large hands, Fr. Jim gently sprinkled water on his forehead. Afterward, his smile spread to everyone there as he proudly held his baptismal candle.

Sr. Dennis Eileen, a Sister of St. Joseph, wrote on her card: *You have my admiration and prayerful support for giving life in Christ and love to Alexander.* Many years later, Alexander would end up sharing his baptism day with the feast day of a wonderful saint, St. John Paul II. It was this saint who wrote, "Through the divine sonship conferred by baptism, it can be said that the Father's words, 'You are my beloved son,' apply to every person baptized and grafted on to Christ."[2]

Yes, our birthday is a very important day, but in the spiritual life, our baptism day is even more important. With our baptism, we have a new family, a new life. After dreaming of, praying for, and now watching Alexander bond with us—his new family in his new life—the sacrament of Baptism took on a whole new meaning. In the many years that have passed, I never miss a baptism to which I am invited.

Through his baptism, Alexander was not just a member of *our* family but now a *forever* member of the family of God. And he had a multitude of godparents. No skimping here. So many of the dear and special friends who had prayed for him and for us—whom I call our prayer warriors—stood by at the font praying, and continue to pray for him throughout his life.

2 John Paul II, "General Audience," April 1, 1998, Libreria Editrice Vaticana, accessed March 18, 2025, https://www.vatican.va/content/john-paul-ii/en/audiences/1998/documents/hf_jp-ii_aud_01041998.html.

One day during his first year home with us, I sat outside on a bench in our front yard looking through the mail. Among the bills and magazines was Alexander's green card. I remember being surprised by its arrival. No one had mentioned it to me, or if they did, it had slipped my mind. I remember that the card actually said *Resident Alien Card* rather than Permanent Resident Card as they do today. The term "resident alien" is applied to any person who has been allowed to live (and work) in the United States without being an American citizen.

With its arrival, Jack and I knew (after a deep sigh) that we had one more governmental step to take, or more accurately, one more major legal milestone to accomplish. We had to ensure that Alexander became a citizen of the United States as soon as possible. Although in our minds he should have automatically been a citizen of our country, our government obviously did not see it the same way. Jack and I began delving into the process of citizenship. However, once again, we learned that our desires often take longer to be realized than we could ever wish for or cause to happen.

The years passed, but at long last Alexander recited the Pledge of Allegiance and became a citizen of the United States when he was in the fourth grade. No longer could he be considered an "alien" or "sojourner" in his country. Jack and I drove Alexander to Charlotte to participate in the ceremony and receive his Certificate of Naturalization. Afterward, we drove him back to St. Leo School where his class and his teacher, Mrs. Elder, were waiting for him with American flags and open arms and hearts. It was a happy and very patriotic day.

For the first year or so, with the approval of our pediatrician, we mostly ignored the two diagnoses of celiac disease and lactose intolerance. This was mainly because Alexander could never get his fill of food. He was always eating. We wanted him to make up for lost time and to put on as much weight as he could. One of the best ways to do this seemed to be through doughnuts.

Although the doughnut had played a crucial supporting role in the adoption process, I saw its true power when it put a smile on his face. His favorite was the Original Glazed, and he and Jack spent many Saturday mornings driving to the local Krispy Kreme when the doughnuts were "Hot Now." He ate as many as he possibly could.

Finally, after letting him eat doughnuts to his heart's content, we had to tackle the diagnosis he had come home with, the one that helped to get Alexander out of Russia and into our home: celiac disease. We had a biopsy done, and, as it turned out, the Russians were correct in their diagnosis (though they were wrong about him having lactose intolerance). Our doctor assured us that with a proper diet and care, he would be just fine.

There were two main difficulties that came with the official diagnosis. The first was simply finding gluten-free food products in a country that had not really heard of or embraced the concept of being gluten free. The second was explaining to the son of a Krispy Kreme Doughnut man that he should no longer eat the doughnuts he had grown accustomed to devouring. Both were ongoing challenges. But fast-forward twenty-five years, and now Alexander's "problem" has become one of the nation's favorite diets! He has his pick of gluten-free foods just about everywhere he goes.

Further evidence that God makes all things new—and apparently gluten free.

17

A Mother's Love

When Jesus saw his mother and the disciple there whom he loved, he said to his mother, "Woman, behold, your son." Then he said to the disciple, "Behold, your mother." And from that hour the disciple took her into his home.

—John 19:26-27

Although God is certainly pleased with the end result, without a doubt He used this journey to change me into the woman I am today. Before, God was "out there somewhere," and I would call upon Him when necessary. Where before complete (or even partial) trust in God's Providence was missing, I have learned that it is the bedrock of hope. I know Him better now, and I trust Him, thanks in large part to His Mother, Our Blessed Mother, Mary.

Mary taught me more about a mother's love than I ever could have imagined. I was looking to rescue a child; she was rescuing me from my own doubt. She revealed to me then, and continues to show me now, that the love of a mother is one of the most important—and essential—gifts one can receive in life. Its value cannot be measured or even fully understood.

A mother's love can be sacrificial, as in the mother who knows that she cannot properly physically, mentally, or financially care for the child she carries in her womb and so chooses to allow someone else to love and raise her child through adoption.

Scripture says that Jesus' Mother, Our Blessed Mother, "was greatly troubled at what was said and pondered what sort of greeting this might be" (Luke 1:29), but her heart was flooded with assurance, and she said yes to God. She became His Mother and, then, at the Cross, ours as well. She walked in faith, and I must too. When I stumble and fall, Mary comes to me and takes me to Jesus, her Son, just as she aided me in my search for my son.

A mother's love is often described as unconditional. A child doesn't have to do or be anything to receive this love. Mary's motherly intercession has helped me to understand that this is how God loves us. Perhaps that is why we must all turn and become like little children in order to enter the kingdom of Heaven. Jesus clearly states: "Amen, I say to you, unless you turn and become like children, you will not enter the kingdom of heaven" (Matt. 18:3).

Like the Blessed Virgin Mary's love for her Son and for each one of us, a mother's love is eternal; it never ends. Our Mother Mary is always with us, watching over us and ready to help *if we just ask her.*

I stayed true to the promise I made to Mary behind the locked bathroom door: *that I would get to know her better*, and through her, her Son, Jesus. Little did I know that my journey to Russia would be just the beginning of my travels. In the many years that have passed since I clutched the holy card on the bathroom floor of my mother-in-law's home, Jack and I have traveled to visit and honor Our Blessed Mother at many pilgrimage and apparition sites around the world. Through my promise made so long ago, the Lord has made our relationship blossom in many wonderful ways.

According to Catholic teaching, Mary was assumed, body and soul, into Heaven. This is the dogma of the Assumption of Mary.

And she has been appearing to us here on earth ever since she left us. Often, the places where she has appeared have become Marian shrines, holy places marking her apparition or some other miracle attributed to her, and, in turn, pilgrimage sites. Pilgrims come seeking a miracle, a healing, or just out of gratitude and the desire to know their Heavenly Mother better. Removed from daily routines and surrounded by old and new friends, they hope to encounter God—and His Mother—in new and wondrous ways.

Our first one didn't even start out as a plan or even a strategy. It was just born of a desire—the desire to *go and see*. Jack and I knew that his mom, whose given name was Bernadette, had always wanted to go to Lourdes. She had often spoken of one day "meeting" and getting to know her namesake, the young girl Our Blessed Mother appeared to on a hillside near the small village of Lourdes, in southern France.

Since Jack's dad had recently passed away, we decided to make this happen for his grieving mom. For me, this was also a special way of thanking his mom for introducing me, by way of a simple prayer card, to the depth of love and hope that comes through a relationship with Our Blessed Mother.

All three of our children were able to spend this time with their grandmother, Bernadette, pushing her wheelchair when it was necessary, or holding her arm or her hand when it wasn't. As we wound our way through the grotto where St. Bernadette first saw Our Blessed Mother, we each touched or drank some of the water that was offered to purify our hearts. It was a very special time with three holy women.

With the first one under our belt, "more" became almost easy, and our desire became almost a holy addiction. During our pilgrimage, "The Footsteps of St. Paul," led by Fr. Dave Pivonka, we traversed all around Greece, as well as to Mt. Koressos, near Ephesus, in modern-day Turkey. Jack and I had our marriage vows renewed at the House of the Virgin Mary, or "Mother Mary's House" in Ephesus. Tradition has it that Our Blessed Mother lived out her final days there with the Apostle John before being assumed into Heaven.

Just as people cautioned us about adopting a child and even going to Russia, many did the same about visiting the Holy Land. Once again we listened to their concerns, but we went anyway. We sort of looked at it as a "rite of passage," especially as Jack and I were growing in our faith. We wanted to see where Our Blessed Mother and her Son walked while they both lived on this earth and where her Son died. We (again!) renewed our marriage vows at a church in Cana, the small city where Jesus turned water into wine—my favorite of His many miracles.

With Fr. Dave once again our leader, we pilgrims walked the Via Dolorosa in Jerusalem, also known as the Way of the Cross, which Jesus walked for us and where His Mother followed Him. Our goal was the Church of the Holy Sepulchre, where Jesus was crucified and which contains His now-empty tomb. This journey of two thousand feet, which is less than half a mile, took much longer and was much harder than I ever imagined. We took turns carrying a real cross, though I'm sure that it was much lighter than the one that Our Lord carried for us. Now when I pray the Stations of the Cross, I have a new perspective, similar to when you pray for or with a friend, because *I know them.*

I am also very grateful that camels aren't our regular mode of transportation. The ride was a bit like sitting in a rocking chair on top of a ladder that is tied to a bicycle. Once was enough.

The reason Jack and I chose the twelfth of December as the date for our wedding was *not* because it was the feast day of Our Lady of Guadalupe. It just happened to be the first Saturday after Jack graduated from Auburn. However, in the many years that have passed, we have come to understand and appreciate not only what an exceptional blessing it was to have celebrated our wedding on this day, but also to celebrate each of our anniversaries as well. This shrine in Mexico City contains the actual *tilma*, or cloak, worn by St. Juan Diego when Our Blessed Mother appeared to him in 1531. Miraculously imprinted on that cloak is the image of Our Blessed Mother. Neither the tilma nor the iridescent image of Our Lady show any signs of deterioration after nearly five hundred years—both miracles in themselves. Now thirty-five years into our marriage, Jack and I were determined to go and understand our wedding feast day, and Fr. Dave agreed to take us.

We were a small group, fifteen total. Inside the glorious Basilica of Our Lady of Guadalupe, there is a moving sidewalk that continuously transports millions of pilgrims past the glowing *tilma* hanging just above for all to see and venerate. Jack and I rode that sidewalk again and again, around and around we went, as many times as years we had been married. Talk about being dizzy!

My mother had recently passed away, and her passing was very difficult. On that pilgrimage to Guadalupe, Our Lady gave me a consolation I will never forget. She is such a true mother, who is present to us down to the least details of our lives.

On the last day of our pilgrimage, we were scheduled to attend Mass at a certain "famous" church, have lunch, and then head to the airport for our flights home. As we gathered in the lobby of the hotel, Fr. Dave informed us that there was a change in plans. We were now walking to Mass at a local parish church just around the corner on February 5th Street.

My head started spinning as I leaned against the lobby wall. *You see, February 5th is the birthday of not only my mother but Jack's mom too!* This change in churches had to be a sign from my many mothers, earthly and heavenly, that *everything was going to be all right.* They would continue to be with us and show us the way.

Of course, I am aware that the reported apparitions at Medjugorje have not been determined to be of supernatural origins. In that, I am a faithful daughter of the Church and await Her decision! Nevertheless, Jack and I decided to visit the small town in Bosnia and Herzegovina to go and see this site for ourselves. By this time, both of our mothers were with Our Heavenly Mother, and though we had received peace and consolation and the sure hope that they were together, we still felt the need and *a longing* to go and pray to honor Our Lady wherever we could do so.

We were there on November 1 and 2, 2016, All Saints Day and All Souls Day, a very special time in the Church calendar. Climbing Cross Mountain in Medjugorje reminded us of our adoption journey. On some parts of the ascent, we hiked somewhat smooth paths and moved relatively quickly and easily. Other parts of the climb up were treacherous, with rocks that would come loose and cause us to stumble. Every so often, the people in front of us would stop or stumble, and we would have to pause or choose an alternate route. While the climb up Cross Mountain was crowded, when we came down a few hours later, our route was almost deserted. And though the rocks were still unreliable and the hike still a bit precarious, the descent was relatively easy and quick.

Our time on top of the mountain was simply glorious. Though the air was cool, the sun shone brightly upon us as we sang songs giving God thanks and praise. We felt we had been invited to this place and to the difficult climb to the top. This is also true of our adoption. It seems strange that God would invite us to *hard things*. Usually, invitations are sent out for events that are fun and easygoing, such as birthday parties and weddings. But Our Lord's invitation to the Heavenly Banquet passes by way of saying "yes" to His call to walk some difficult roads in this life. After all, He knows our hearts better than we do.

Everyone said we had to go to Fatima. We weren't sure why; you cannot know until you go. Perhaps it was because of the beauty, complexity, and mystery surrounding Our Blessed Mother's message, which involved secrets, prophecy, and revelations. The "Miracle of the Sun" was also very intriguing.

However, as we prepared for our trip and learned about Fatima, perhaps we needed to go because Our Lady had called for the consecration of Russia to her Immaculate Heart in one of the Fatima apparitions, and which St. John Paul II *actually did* in 1984. A few years later, Communism collapsed throughout Eastern Europe and the USSR ceased to be. A short ten years later, we traveled to Russia as a family to find our son. The more we learned about the pilgrimage site, the more we developed a deep and personal connection to this amazing place.

In 1917, Mary appeared to three young shepherd children in the small village of Fatima, Portugal. Lucia (age ten), Francisco (age nine), and Jacinta (age seven) received several visits on the thirteenth of the month, during which Our Blessed Mother shared visions, prophecies, and secrets. She also exhorted the children to "pray the Rosary every day." Her final visit included a visible miracle where the sun appeared to "dance around" and "zig-zag" in the sky, lovingly known as the "Miracle of the Sun." Thousands of people were there to witness this miracle, many of whom arrived as skeptics but left with a radical shift in their thoughts and beliefs.

Each night in Fatima, from April to October, there is a candlelight procession where a statue of Our Blessed Mother is carried through the square of the beautifully illuminated basilica. Four men were needed to carry Our Lady. Upon arriving at our hotel, Jack and three others from our pilgrim group were invited to carry Our Lady that evening. It was the eve of the Assumption of Our Blessed Mother into Heaven, so this night was a big deal in Fatima. It was a big deal to Jack and me too. That was the prayer we had prayed for our son, "Lovely Lady Dressed in Blue." And Our Lady had answered.

We know there is still much to learn about Our Blessed Mother, most especially how much she loves and continuously cares for us, longing for us to know and love her Son. Each one of these pilgrimages was a very special and beautiful experience and provided an invitation to grow in personal holiness and in the perfection that God desires.

So many of the details of these religious excursions have faded away, but the sacred experiences remain with me and have forever shaped my heart and my life. I have developed a deeper relationship with Our Blessed Mother and found healing during these pilgrimages that help me *to love, give, suffer, and offer* continuously, just as she did during her earthly life and continues to do from Heaven. Little did I know that she had been with me all along. Her desire was for me to *see* the Father's will unfold in my life and to help me make my life one long "yes" to God. Thank you, Lovely Lady Dressed in Blue, for *teaching me how to pray and for showing me the way* to your Son, Jesus.

Through all my journeys, I have come to understand that *life is a pilgrimage.* All of us are on a journey. I hope that we notice and experience God along the way and are open to being graced with struggles, surprises, crosses, gifts, joys, and sorrows until we finally come face-to-face with the One Whom we long to see. Jesus told us, "I am the way and the truth and the life. No one comes to the Father except through me" (John 14:6).

18

Spirit of Adoption

We are not the sum of our weaknesses and failures; we are the sum of the Father's love for us and our real capacity to become the image of his Son.

—Pope St. John Paul II

During our ten days in Russia, I witnessed Russian soldiers in tall fur hats marching in Red Square. I used what remained of the only toilet in a large Russian orphanage and spent time in an old, dilapidated Russian hospital. I was presented with a gold medal on a blue ribbon and kissed on both cheeks by the director of adoptions in Moscow. I was called a hero by a Russian stranger and had my picture taken only because I was American. I felt the fear of wondering if my family and I would ever make it home. But above and beyond all of this, I witnessed the pure joy of a little boy seeing *his* family for the first time in his life.

What is unbelievable to me now is that it wasn't until I was in my early thirties that I ever even thought about people being orphans. In our current American culture, the word *orphan* is simply not part of our everyday vocabulary; it is most often only romanticized in stories such as *Little Orphan Annie* or *Anne of Green Gables.*

And yet, we encounter the orphan, which was of course common in the ancient world, throughout the Scriptures. Here we read that we, too, are *adopted children* of God:

> But when the fullness of time had come, God sent his Son, born of a woman, born under the law, to ransom those under the law, so that we might receive adoption. As proof that you are children, God sent the spirit of his Son into hearts, crying out, "Abba, Father!" So you are no longer a slave but a child, and if a child then also an heir, through God. (Gal. 4:4–7)

But do we really understand the significance of passages like the one above? If we are largely unfamiliar with adoption as a culture, can we appreciate the weight and significance of such a statement?

After our journey through the adoption process, I believe that I can. And yet it wasn't until years later that I came to fully realize the *theological* implications of St. Paul's words above—words that carry so much meaning about our dignity and our destiny as God's children.

I remember exactly where I was when I first heard this biblical understanding of adoption spoken of by author Mike Aquilina, cofounder of the St. Paul Center for Biblical Theology. Mike had been invited to come and speak on Archangel Radio, our local Catholic radio station, and was staying with us at our home. Mike recounted that at the time of Jesus, the Romans considered adopted children as precious—even more precious than biological children—because they had been *chosen* by their parents. As I sat listening in the living room, I was stunned. *Why had I never heard this before?*

In the Roman Empire during the time of Jesus, astonishingly, biological parents were allowed to disown their biological children for any reason. If the parent-child relationship was not desired by a parent, it did not have to be permanent.

For the Romans, however, adoption had a very powerful significance. When one adopted a child, this meant that this child was desired by the parents—that is, he or she was *freely chosen.* The adopted child was given a new identity—one that made him or her a sharer in all the possessions and responsibilities of the family. According to Roman law, unlike a biological child, an adopted child could never be disowned; he or she was a permanent member of the family. They were elevated to a position far beyond that of a biological child. *Wow.*

As a Roman citizen, St. Paul would have known this, which explains why he so often compares the adoption of a child to our own adoption as God's sons and daughters. As a further example, to show his Roman audience what it meant to be a child of God, he used a reality with which they were familiar when he wrote:

> For those who are led by the Spirit of God are children of God. For you did not receive a spirit of slavery to fall back into fear, but you received a *spirit of adoption*, through which we cry, "*Abba, Father!*" The Spirit itself bears witness with our spirit that we are children of God, and if children, then heirs, heirs of God and joint heirs with Christ, if only we suffer with him so that we may also be glorified with him. (Rom. 8:14–17, emphasis mine)

St. Paul uses and refers to the practice of adoption to convey a spiritual truth that is as relevant today as it was two thousand years ago: through the gift of the Holy Spirit given at our baptism, all of us are adopted children of the triune God, Father, Son, and Holy Spirit.

Fr. Dave explains this truth beautifully in his book *Breath of God*. Jesus, the Son, invites us into the relationship He has with the Father, His *Abba* (which has the sense of "daddy" in Aramaic). The Holy Spirit—the Breath of God—reveals to us that Jesus' Father is *our* Father too.[3]

By virtue of our baptism, we are adopted sons and daughters of God the Father. And by Jesus' Passion, death, and rising from the dead, we are no longer separated or *alienated* from God but heirs of His household, where there are many rooms prepared for us.

> In my Father's house there are many dwelling places. If there were not, would I have told you that I am going to prepare a place for you? And if I go and prepare a place for you, I will come back again and take you to myself, so that where I am you also may be. (John 14:2–3)

And God remains with us—remains—isn't that amazing? And His Blessed Mother too. She is our Mother and is always watching over us, hearing our prayers and interceding for us, just as I truly believe she interceded for me on behalf of my son.

As a grandmother now, I look back and reflect on how I raised my children. Because we live close to each other, I am able to participate in the process of my children raising their children. There are times that I sweat, pray, and beg God that *everything will be all right*. But mostly I relish and rejoice in the amazing moments where I thank God, Our Blessed Mother, and all the saints for their grace, intercessions, and prayers as things turn out not just okay, but wonderful.

[3] Fr. Dave Pivonka, T.O.R., *Breath of God* (Notre Dame: Ave Maria Press, 2015), 81.

Perhaps that is why Jesus gave His Mother to us when He hung on the Cross. We need her help as we and those we love navigate this earthly pilgrimage.

I have come to understand that God the Father is only fully revealed through Jesus, Who is "God with us." Jesus came to share His Father with us and invite us to be a part of their family as true children—*fully adopted children of God*—and so we are all able to call God, "Abba, Father," just as Jesus did.

I am living proof. For if God would heed my pleas, tears, and clenched fists despite my distrust, there is proof that He truly is a loving Father. But the greater evidence is in my ongoing conversion, my deepening surrender, my growing devotion. He gave me a son, but even more, He continually, miraculously, gives me Himself.

He desires that for all of us. And He has a plan for all of us, a plan for our restoration and well-being. To bring it about, like a loving parent, God will pursue us to the end—never forcing but *always coming*. He will run to us, like the father in the story of the Prodigal Son. He will search for us, like the shepherd who leaves the ninety-nine to go in search of the one who was lost. He will go to the ends of the earth (yes, even Russia) and the darkest recesses of our interior world to find us and *bring us home*: this is what He did for me. When we feel alone, when we are tempted to feel "orphaned" in spirit, we can remember the trust of the little boy in Russia who knew *with confidence* that his parents were coming for him. That is exactly the way our God wants us to believe in His love for us—His everlasting, relentless love.

Afterword

Where We Are Now

Behold, I make all things new.

—Revelation 21:5

To this day, when people complain about a bathroom's toilet paper or lack thereof, either Jack or I will say, "Well, you could use old magazines or newspapers."

They look at us like we are crazy, and maybe they are right. But, I promise you, we have never again taken toilet paper for granted—especially Jack.

But it wasn't merely our perspective of basic necessities that was changed, but of life. Through our journey of infertility, and then adoption, we enriched our own lives as well as our son's—and perhaps we even made a difference in this difficult and doubting world of ours. We are living proof that scriptural truisms like serving the orphan and the alien are not merely suggestions. Certainly these commands of Scripture generally—Jesus' words in particular—have a spiritual meaning or interpretation, but they are also seeds that God can and will plant in many hearts as long as there are children in need. In allowing that seed to grow, Jack and I served the orphan and the alien in one person, saving two birds with one stone, so to speak.

I am not saying that we did anything braver or wiser than many people do every day, but we did do something that many people told us was risky and foolish. Now, as I look back, I wouldn't have had it any other way:

> God chose the foolish of the world to shame the wise, and God chose the weak of the world to shame the strong, and God chose the lowly and despised of the world, those who count for nothing, to reduce to nothing those who are something, so that no human being might boast before God. (1 Cor. 1:27–29)

In other words, Jack and I, foolish and weak as we were, were open to going and getting one of those whom the world had forgotten but in the eyes of God was loved and prized. God gave us the courage we needed because we did not fully know just what we were undertaking.

Jack has been retired from Krispy Kreme for many years now, and we have since moved to his home state of Alabama. Lauren married Dan Johnson in 2007, and Jennifer married Philip Martin in 2009. So far, they have blessed us with twelve grandchildren on earth and three in Heaven, and we enjoy being an active part of their lives.

During the summer of 2020, as the COVID-19 virus ravaged our world and sent everyone into isolation, I found myself at home with a lot of time on my hands. My son-in-law Philip, a writer and teacher, was also available, as many of his activities and responsibilities had been significantly altered. Grateful for this time (and his talents), I was determined to put both to good use. Together, Philip and I poured over my notes and journals, retelling the story God had begun so long ago.

The year 2020 also marked twenty-five years since we had traveled to Russia to adopt Alexander. For me it was a milestone—a quarter of a century had gone by and so many loved ones had left this world for the next. I knew it was important to tell the story of how his adoption happened and the change that God had wrought in me, and now seemed to be the right time to tell this story—at least get it down on paper.

While I began writing, Alexander was beginning a new journey too. As so many blessings come from difficult circumstances, the COVID pandemic, by forcing folks inside, caused Alexander to go online to CatholicMatch.com, where he met the love of his life, Laura.

In April of 2022, Fr. Dave married Alex and Laura at St. Rita Catholic Church in New Orleans. Just shy of one year later, Jack and I traveled back there to await the birth of their first child, a boy who was to be named Simon.

However, Alexander was in control of this journey and this story; he was now texting us, inviting us to *come to him*. We met him at the hospital.

The hallways were mostly empty and quiet, just like the hallways of the orphanage in Podolsk buried deep in our memories. Like many institutions, this older hospital exhibited a sterile quality reminiscent of the place Jack and I had wandered in once before looking for Alexander. Memories began flooding my mind and my emotions; having already been triggered by the excitement of meeting a new grandson, they began to explode. As Jack and I swept through cold metal doors and veered around corners, I kept reminding myself that this time, in these God-filled moments, although we were once again looking for our son, and although Alexander once again was waiting on and looking for us, this time we would be meeting *his son*, our grandson, for the first time.

We gently pushed through the final door, and there was Alexander holding Simon, his son. We had found them: our son and our thirteenth grandchild.

One day his children will have questions for him, and my prayer is that this book will allow him to answer those questions in the best way possible. However, the most important reason this book is written is that I wanted him to know how much he was, is, and will forever be *loved*.

About the Author

Although she grew up Lutheran, it wasn't until college that Jamie McAleer first accepted Jesus into her heart. It was then that she met her husband, Jack, and converted to Catholicism. Both Jamie and Jack were major players in the growth of Krispy Kreme Doughnut Corporation. They have served as board members of Legatus, Lifeteen, and Franciscan University of Steubenville. After retiring to Alabama, they helped create 4PM Media and 10th Hour Productions to give thanks to God for their many blessings—especially for their children and many grandchildren.